D0897835

# SECRETS

## — OF A —

# TAX FREE
# LIFE

### Surprising Write-Off Strategies
### Most Business Owners Miss

Featuring America's Top Certified Tax Coaches
Foreword by Dominique Molina, CPA CTC

Published by Certified Tax Coach,™ LLC, San Diego, CA

Certified Tax Coach™ is a registered trademark
Printed in the United States of America.
ISBN: 978-0-9832341-1-1

This publication is designed to provide accurate and authoritative information with regard to the subject matter covered. It is sold with the understanding that the publisher is not engaged in rendering legal, accounting, or other professional advice. If legal advice or other expert assistance is required, the services of a competent professional should be sought. The opinions expressed by the authors in this book are not endorsed by Certified Tax Coach™ and are the sole responsibility of the author rendering the opinion.

This title is available at special quantity discounts for bulk purchases for sales promotions, premiums, fundraising, and educational use. Special versions or book excerpts can also be created to fit specific needs.

For more information, please write:
Certified Tax Coach™
7676 Hazard Center Dr Ste 500
San Diego, CA 92108
or call 1.888.582.9752
Visit us online at www.CertifiedTaxCoach.com

# TABLE OF CONTENTS

# FOREWORD

## By Dominique Molina, CPA CTC

I've spent many years as a practicing CPA honing my skills, working with businesses of all sizes, seeking out the top tax strategies and coaching others to achieve maximum results. One thing I've noticed is no matter the size of the business, everyone is actively trying to get ahead. Young or old, experienced or just starting out, each person strives for a piece of the American Dream. Somewhere within each of us lies the belief that if we work hard, our wealth will grow and our results will pay off in the end.

There are two basic concepts in aspiring to make more money. First, you can seek to earn more. Yet this presents a challenge as most people are seeking to earn more, yet most rarely do so. This is especially challenging now, in difficult economic times. The harsh reality may be that you are watching your earnings dwindle. Layoffs are rampant, and Americans find themselves doing more and making less as employers struggle to stay afloat with pay cuts and work furloughs. Seeking to earn more is an arduous and unpredictable process. What will you do? How will you do it? When will you do it? You can say you'd like to earn more money, but the question is, "can you earn more money?" On the other hand, you can choose a defensive approach. Financial defense is spending less. For most Americans, taxes are our biggest expense.

Therefore, it makes sense to focus your financial defense where you spend the most. Financial defense, particularly in the area of tax planning guarantees results. You can spend all sorts of time, effort, and money promoting your business or working towards promotions at work. But that can't guarantee results.

So how do you reduce your tax and keep more of what you earn? Or even better, how can you earn more without paying tax? These questions can be answered by looking to the wisest investors and financial experts for advice.

One of the most interesting times of year for me, comes when famed Billionaire, Warren Buffet, announces the percentage of tax he pays in comparison to his secretary. You may be surprised to discover that it is the humble secretary, earning just $60,000 each year in salary, who pays almost twice the tax rate of one of the world's wealthiest men.

How can this be? Is it positive proof of all the rumors that the wealthy pay very little tax while the burden of providing for our government falls on the middle class? And why does Mr. Buffet disclose this secret to the public?

Warren Buffet discloses this information to the public to demonstrate that owning a business and taking advantage of every available break is the best way to increase your wealth. Business owners have the most opportunity to create cash and wealth from an idea rather than a task. Even better, they have the most loopholes, deductions, credits, and tax breaks available for them. This combination of benefits creates the possibility to earn more and keep more through tax planning.

The reason the wealthy pay less in tax is not because of how much money they earn. Rather it is because of how they earn it. It is a myth that the rich pay less in tax simply because they are rich. They pay less in tax because they have knowledge; and they can afford the right team of people to provide the secrets to paying less. You can do what the rich do by learning these secrets and having a plan for keeping more of what you earn. Owning a business provides the method and unlocks the door to limitless ideas of reducing your tax bill.

I speak all across the country teaching people how to use tax planning as a way to keep more of what they earn. When preparing for my media appearances, I always have to chuckle when a show producer instructs me not to use the word, "loopholes." There is a common misconception that someone using tax planning or loopholes is a shady person, or someone practicing tax avoidance. The truth is that loopholes are created by the government. They want us to use loopholes. Loopholes are just government incentives to promote its public policy.

Most loopholes exist for business owners. More deductions, breaks, and credits exist for business owners because business is the heart of our economy. By providing breaks to businesses, our government can stimulate the economy and keep it flourishing in times of good, and fuel it in recessions.

This is especially evident now, in our troubled economic times. We can clearly see Washington's stimulus geared toward businesses because small business employs people, invests in equipment and capital resources, and creates general movement of cash in our economy. In a sense, providing breaks to businesses helps to jump-start our economy. Since the government wants our economy to grow, they design the majority of stimulus aid toward business to create a change in our economic climate.

Why not jump-start your own economy by using the loopholes available to you through tax planning? At the end of the day, if you're serious about getting your business to succeed, and you want to make the most of your tax plan, you're going to need some help. Nobody can be an expert at everything, and the tax code is complicated. Make sure you work with someone who not only has good knowledge of the tax code and filing requirements, but who will work with you proactively throughout the year to make sure you are taking advantage of every available break. A good proactive advisor includes someone who routinely brings you new ideas to save money. If your current advisor is not regularly talking to you about tax strategies, it's time for a new one! Do not limit yourself to working with someone face-to-face. Modern technology provides many opportunities to work with the RIGHT advisor, even if that person is across the country, instead of across the street.

The authors of this book are some of the top Certified Tax Coaches across the country; experts in the art of paying less tax. They are tax professionals who scour the tax code and thoroughly examine their client's income and business options to rescue every deduction, tax advantage, and credit possible. Certified Tax Coaches emphasize year-round proactive planning to ensure that business owners can utilize every available loophole and savings opportunity possible; and they've come together to share these secrets with you.

The strategies in this book will help teach you how to use the tax code to your advantage. No, you don't have to be a billionaire like Buffet to pay very little in tax; you just need to know the secrets.

Here's to teaching you the Secrets of a Tax Free Life,

> Dominique Molina, CPA CTC
> President
> The American Institute of Certified Tax Coaches

# CHAPTER ONE

# The Single Most Expensive Tax Mistake People Make

### By Joseph Conrad, EA CTC

*"There are two kinds of failures: Those who thought and never did, and those who did and never thought."*

**—Laurence J. Peter**

The IRS believes that at least 80% of taxpayers overpay their taxes. It gets even worse if you are a business owner or an employee with income over $125,000!

According to the Small Business Administration, more than 50% of small businesses fail within the first 12 months! Given these staggering odds, it's more important than ever not to overpay your taxes, wasting critical cash that should stay in your pocket. Even after 30 years of tax services to individuals and businesses, I am still amazed how hard people work to make a profit yet how easily they give it up in taxes to the government.

If you're going to waste an excessive amount of your money overpaying your taxes, why not throw it away on a new boat, helicopter, or airplane, with a Plan for it? At least with a new boat you could '**Plan and Play**' instead of **giving it away!**

You did not start a business or choose a particular career without a plan, you should approach paying your taxes the same. Keep in mind, however, not all tax planning is the same.

# Five Levels of Tax Planning

1. No Tax Planning
2. Power Planning
3. Rear View Mirror Planning
4. Good Tax Planning
5. GREAT Tax Planning

## No Tax Planning

This is pretty self-explanatory. Year after year Uncle Sam has readily accepted taxpayers' overpayments as a result of no tax planning. Instead of having their money used to bail out car companies and financial institutions, taxpayers could have easily funded their own retirement plans, college educations, vacation homes, etc. with savings from tax planning tools. Too often, their reasoning is, "I'll just work harder and earn more money. Eventually, I'll have everything I want." Unfortunately, the more they make, the more they owe. It's not as if the tax code is set up with a cap and after reaching a certain dollar amount, they've paid enough. It is a percentage of everything you earn, unless you plan.

## Power Planning

I refer to Power Planning as the type of tax advice driven by power tools, be it a mower, a blower or any other engine-powered machine. Power Planning is a self-implemented tax strategy from the Guru of tax advice, your brother-in-law's lawn care person or his neighborhood fix-it man. Your brother-in-law Bob, got a piece of hot tax advice from his faithful Lawn-Guy and believing it to be a hush-hush way around the tax laws and felt it essential, he passed it along to you. Your radar should go off here for two reasons. First, it's hush-hush advice, which means it most likely won't stand up legally. Second, if the Lawn-Guy is such an expert on tax law... why is he mowing lawns for a living? Perhaps it's his passion? (Sense my sarcasm?)

Before we dismiss it completely, let's take a look at the Lawn-Guy's tax advice.

Lawn-Guy told Bob he can write-off a boat, airplane, motorhome, trailer, etc. if it had 'sleeping and plumbing,' meaning a self-contained unit that he can live in. Bob *knew* this was true because he heard someone at the fast food joint talking about the big motorhome *he* had just purchased, which his accountant said he *could* write-off on his taxes.

That was all Bob needed to hear. He was off to the dealer to purchase the motorhome he had dreamt about for so long. First thing Monday morning, Bob called payroll and adjusted his W2 withholdings to compensate for the new monthly payment from his tax write-off. "I'm a guy of action," Bob tells all his friends, co-workers, and anyone else that will listen to him.

Eventually, Bob marches into his Tax Guy the last week in March. Bob is an early filer, none of this April 15th stuff for him. He was certain he would be congratulated for making his brilliant tax strategy purchase.

Bob soon learned two things. First, he only gets to write-off the interest paid on his motor home loan which equaled $18,000. Second, his write-off does not reduce his taxes dollar for dollar. Bob's $18,000 write-off reduced his taxes by $5,940 ($18,000 x 33% tax bracket). Meanwhile, Bob's W2 withholdings had been reduced by $26,400 (all the money he spent this year on his motor home). Now he owed $20,460 ($26,400 - $5,940) more in taxes than he did the year before. So much for the dream of cruising the countryside with ease. Now Bob must figure out where to get the money for his large tax bill and rethink whose tax advice he uses.

## Rear View Mirror Tax Planning

Tax *Preparation* is not the same thing as Tax *Planning*! After-the-fact tax preparation is simply processing a stack of receipts on April 15th and filling in the blanks on a tax return. It is an incomplete service for most business owners and taxpayers.

At some point in time you have probably played a starring role in this scenario. You drop off your receipts at TaxGuy's office and his staff puts all the stuff in the right boxes on the right forms. They work hard to make sure you have what you say you are deducting so there will be no trouble with the IRS. They do not really have any option to DO any planning because planning must be done ahead of time. It is impossible to change the past. Once December 31st of each year is over, you can't change history. Anything that you could do to reduce your taxes is done, finished, gone. Rear View Mirror work is the most popular, and the IRS's favorite because it significantly contributes to the statistic that 80% of people overpay Uncle Sam.

## Good Tax Planning

The last two types of tax planning are the best but it's important to understand the difference between *Good* Tax Planning and *Great* Tax Planning. Anyone can tell you to spend $30,000 on equipment and supplies for the coming year and call that Year-End Tax Planning. That $30,000 tax write-off could save you as much as $12,000 in taxes. That means the government paid for $12,000 of your equipment and supplies. This 40% discount for your business sounds *good* because you were only out-of-pocket $18,000. This type of year-end tweaking is an important part of *good* tax planning but it could be better.

For instance, any time your bank balance goes *down* it often becomes more about cash flow than tax reduction. No matter how good it looks, it may not fit into the budget at that moment. This is one of the biggest reasons taxpayers do not do Tax Planning. Who wants to spend money when something else more pressing looms over them?

## Great Tax Planning

Great Tax Planning has two levels. First, finding tax savings on *money you are already spending.* Second, finding tax savings *without spending any additional money.* Both are possible.

### Money you are already spending.

These are tax savings you find as a result of missed or overlooked tax deductions. This generally requires looking things over and getting a better understanding of the IRS's playbook for maximum tax reductions to increase money in your pocket. These type of deductions fall into two categories, 'Grey zone' and 'Playbook' tax deductions.

## Grey zone tax deductions.

These are deductions you hope and pray the IRS does not ask about or see.

An example of a Grey zone deduction would be placing an inflated value of $1,000 on a 10-year-old business suit worth $100 at a thrift store. Someone in the Grey Zone, then deducts, this value as a charitable deduction. As long as the IRS does not look or ask, many people think it's a great tax deduction because they are acting like the Big Guys and getting away with something. But if the IRS does look, they will not be happy, and you can be certain there will be an adjustment to the tax return.

## Playbook tax deductions.

These are time-tested tax strategies.

An example of a Playbook deduction would be the use of medical expense deductions many taxpayers do not benefit from. If you know how, you can write-off 100% of your medical expenses, regardless of your income level or the 7.5% haircut most itemizers get blasted with. Let me explain that further.

Most taxpayers lose their medical expense deductions from what is known as the 7.5% haircut rule, which went into effect with the Tax Simplification Act of 1986. Basically, your income gets multiplied by 7.5%. To net you any tax savings your medical expense must be larger than that number, otherwise, your medical expenses go on the form... but yield no tax savings. Yes, that's right, no tax savings! By the way, that percentage is slated to go up to 10% with the new tax code. Let's look at an example. Say you earn $100,000 each year and you also have $8,000 each year in medical expenses. Under the current rules, you would only be eligible to deduct $500 of medical expenses because you lose $7,500 under the haircut. (If you ask me that sounds like a buzz cut!)

However, if you own a small business (the thing America is made of), you will be in the same boat and lose your medical expenses deductions completely just like everyone else, UNLESS you make one change. A small business owner can implement a MERP (Medical Expense Reimbursement Plan). This becomes a 100% write-off for the business and helps get around the haircut rules I've described above. All this is in the IRS Playbook and time tested. You can read more about this strategy in Chapter Ten of this book.

## Without Spending Money

One easy example of this type of *great* Tax Planning is called entity selection. This really just means how you are registered as a legal company; Corporation, S-Corporation, Partnership, Sole Proprietor, etc. This affects how you play the game and how much you pay in taxes. There are a lot of different choices with Entities but this one is easy to explain as a simple example.

An example of entity selection is UpDraft Tourguides. UpDraft Tourguides is a partnership. Because the business owner chose to be taxed as a partnership the husband and wife owners have been paying their normal amount of taxes, which includes $22,000 in Self Employment Tax, each year, year after year.

In great tax planning, we suggest they change the type of business entity they use to run UpDraft. This one change reduces their Self Employment tax by approximately $11,000 in the first year. Over five years that's a savings of $55,000, they were previously wasting! This required no change in the way the company does business and no additional money spent draining the cash flow on anything. You can read more about using entity selection in Chapter Six of this book.

This is an example of what we call **Knowing the Rules and Using the Tools.** That is my favorite type of tax planning—Great Tax Planning. It is an instant pay raise, and a wonderful immediate boost to cash flow and business management, without spending any money.

# Place Your Bet—and Win, Guaranteed!

If you could place a bet on a horse and know it was going to win (guaranteed), would you do it?

Once you have that thought solid in your mind consider this: "What would be a great percentage return on investment for that horse? Double your money? Triple your money?"

If you bought a stock such as Apple which is worth three times what you paid for it just three years ago, how would you feel about your choice? You'd think you were pretty smart, and you'd tell all your friends. You probably could not keep it a secret.

Whether you bet on the horse or buy the stock, there is no guarantee you will win big, at least not legally.

Great Tax Planning, on the other hand has a guaranteed outcome. The rulebook says, "Do this and you will get that." It's not a guessing game. The only thing holding most people back is they're so busy working on their business they cannot take the time to sharpen the saw (at least that's what they tell themselves). Their thought process is if they just make more money it will eventually work out. I'll just keep working and someday I will end up with something in the bank. As I mentioned earlier, your tax obligations are based on a percentage of everything you earn.

Great Tax Planning does take skill. It's Greek to people who are not constantly talking the language. That's why you work with a great tax planner—for the guarantee.

But, when you strategically restructure the way your business handles it's deductions, it's not a guessing game. The numbers will work out, the horse will win, the stock price will reach a 300-400% gain, no question. It is not a leap of faith. It's a leap of time and expertise. How much are you willing to spend on great, proactive strategies to earn an ROI of 400%? Leave it to the experts while you concentrate on what you do best. Tax planning will do just that. So give it a try! Plan and Play instead of giving it away.

# Joseph Conrad, EA CTC

Joseph Conrad is the founder and President of JCC, Inc., a strategic tax and business-consulting firm which offers service to the exceptional.

Joseph Conrad has over 22 years of experience as a Small Business Expert, consultant, speaker, and author, who practices the concept of 'GREAT' Tax Planning. His diverse knowledge and experience allows him to bring new and innovative ideas to his clients, while speaking in plain English.

When it comes to saving you tax dollars Joseph uses the analogy from the movie "The Blind." The Quarterback is the highest paid player on the team. YOU are the Quarterback of your team. Joseph (the tax guy) is your left tackle, the second highest paid player on the team. His job is to protect your blind side from the IRS while saving you as many tax dollars as possible. To put up an IRON WALL from what YOU, the Quarterback, will not see coming.

Using ROCK SOLID (tested) strategies right from the IRS playbook. Not wild, hold your breath and hope nobody looks methods. Audit tested real world tax savings that keep your money in YOUR POCKET...

When you bring Joseph onto your team, you can feel confident that you are partnering with a professional who is honest and reliable and who will always have your best interest in mind.

His clients live all across the country.

You can contact Joseph by phone at: (425) 251-8318 or by email at: taxplan@conradtax.com

# CHAPTER TWO

# Things Your Accountant Forgot to Tell You!

### BY CRAIG HAWKINS, CPA CTC

Your CPA or accountant should be one of your most trusted advisors. Literally, you rely on him or her to keep you out of jail, or at least keep the IRS off your back. Implied in your relationship with your accountant is that you will receive professional advice with two specific goals:

1. To help you meet your Federal & State tax obligations
2. To help you pay only the tax required, and no more!

It may be hard for you to believe that your trusted advisor would "forget" to tell you something.

## How is it Possible for My Accountant to Forget to Tell Me?

United States Secretary of Defense Donald Rumsfeld's explanation of the difficulties faced in Iraq was ridiculed, as an abuse of language, when he said:

*"[T]here are known knowns; there are things we know we know. We also know there are known unknowns; that is to say we know there are some things we do not know. But there are also unknown unknowns—the ones we don't know we don't know."*

Donald Rumsfeld's statement caused confusion just like the IRS Tax Code continues to cause confusion today. But in contrast to the IRS code, his statement contains a profound truth. **"Unknown unknowns" are dangerous and costly.** Donald Rumsfeld's "unknown unknowns" cost lives, money and his reputation.

In the area of taxes, potential costly "unknown unknowns" become "knowns" when the **right questions get answered**. For example, "Can your spouse help in the business?," "Do you own a pool?" or "Where have you been finding new customers?" These types of questions help provide information to the advisor so he or she can recommend tax saving opportunities.

Your accountant *cannot forget* to ask all the right questions necessary to explore your tax saving possibilities. Could forgotten questions and forgotten deductions be costing you $5,000 a year? $15,000 a year? $150,000 a year? Maybe more?

Let's test your current accountant and see if anything was forgotten:

# Is a Swimming Pool Just a Swimming Pool or a Powerful Tax Break?

A swimming pool can be a classic example of applying tax code generally used by larger businesses and applying it to a small business. Most small business owners would assume their home swimming pool is not a tax write-off. However, IRS Code Section 132 (j)(4) allows an employer to deduct the cost and maintenance of a gym or athletic facility located on the employer's premises. If the facility is operated by the employer, and substantially used by employer's employees, employees' spouses, and employees' dependents it qualifies as a tax deduction. Facilities would include swimming pool, tennis court, and fitness equipment.

IRS Regulations §1.132-1 adds a twist by indicating that athletic facilities need not be located on the employer's business premises in all cases.

Here's an example to make this easier to understand. Mark the Geologist is the only employee of his "S" Corporation. Mark designates the pool area in his home as the athletic facility available to all "S" Corporation employees. The pool is only used by Mark, his spouse and his kids. Given proper documentation, Mark and his "S" Corporation meet the requirements of IRS Code Section 132 (j)(4). The pool maintenance costs would be deductible as business expenses to the "S" Corporation.

Has your accountant forgotten to tell you that your pool is not just a pool? You may have an employer maintained athletic facility and a great way to reduce your tax!

# Free Money From the IRS!

Are you willing to let the IRS give you $175,000, with the condition that you pay the IRS back $75,000 in five years? Under current law, something like that is possible.

A Closely-Held Insurance Company (CHIC) is a bona fide property/casualty insurance company that you can establish to manage risk in your primary business or professional practice.

Presuming the following conditions:

- Your business is good and will continue to be good for five years.
- You want to accumulate money for retirement or leave a legacy for your family.
- You can put away $100,000 a year for 5 years.
- You are in a 35% tax bracket.

Consider forming a Closely-Held Insurance Company (CHIC) and taking the following steps:

1. Determine what business risk your business has, that CHIC could insure. (For this example: Key Customer Loss Protection)
2. Form your insurance company.
3. Have your business buy Key Customer Loss Protection Insurance from your insurance company with an annual premium of $100,000.

4.  Deduct $100,000 on your business tax return as a Liability Insurance, saving approximately $35,000 each year for five years. Total income tax savings is $175,000. Note your insurance company receives the $100,000 premium tax free because it is a qualified CHIC.

5.  Have your insurance company pay the operating costs and invest the balance in something that is tax free or grows tax deferred.

6.  Liquidate the insurance company after five years. Presuming the investment return earns only enough to cover the CHIC operating costs over the five years; the CHIC would liquidate for a value of $500,000.

7.  Pay the IRS $75,000, ($500,000 x 15% = $75,000). The owner of the insurance company would receive $500,000 taxed at long term capital gains rates, currently 15%.

The maximum insurance premium possible is $1,200,000, per CHIC, per year.

A CHIC is also a powerful estate tax tool. The CHIC requires limited start-up costs and can be owned by children or grandchildren. The CHIC's value would not be included in the decedent's estate if already owned by an heir. In the example above, $500,000 of taxable estate would have been moved to the heirs free from estate tax and generation skipping transfer tax. Presuming 35% estate tax, an additional savings of $175,000 is created for those with taxable estates.

As you can see, the CHIC strategy is an attractive way to create tax savings. Although I have simplified the rules in my explanation above, you should select a strong advisor with expertise in this complicated area to assist you. But the results can be amazing!

# Rent My House to Myself – Why?

IRS Publication 17 indicates "If you use a dwelling unit as a home and you rent it fewer than 15 days during the year, do not include any rental income in your income. Also, you cannot deduct any expenses as rental expenses."

If you are one of the lucky ones that live in a city that is hosting a Super Bowl, consider planning your vacation for the two weeks around the Super Bowl and renting your house out for some exorbitant fee. If you rent your home out for less than 15 days the rental fee is tax free. Last time the Super Bowl was held in Tampa, the rental fees could have easily paid for a nice vacation.

Other than the Super Bowl, you may also consider renting your house out to your business for business functions such as:

- Board Meetings
- Client Appreciation Events
- A Video or Commercial Shoot Location
- Network or Marketing Events

If you did rent your home to your business for a board meeting, the business would deduct the rental fee as a business deduction and you would not be required to report the income on your personal return.

If you have a second home , vacation home, boat or RV that qualify as "Dwelling Unit Used as a Home" as defined by the IRS all units can be rented tax free for up to 14 days each.

# Expensive Hobby or Marketing Costs?

I was once asked by a client, "If I buy a trailer to haul my son Mike's motocross bike to races and I put my company logo on the trailer, what can I deduct?" A typical accountant might say either the cost of the logos or both the trailer and logos.

An accountant making sure that nothing is forgotten would ask more questions:

**Accountant:** Do you get business from your son's motocross racing?

**Taxpayer:** Yes, I have gotten lots of new business from supporting Mike's motocross team.

**Accountant:** Would you get more business if you bought the trailer with the logos and continued to sponsor Mike's racing?

**Taxpayer:** Yes, that's why I am considering it.

**Accountant:** Is it fair to say that the primary reason you are buying the trailer and sponsoring Mike's racing is to earn more business?

**Taxpayer:** I would not do it otherwise.

**Accountant:** If the IRS were to ask, could you document enough additional sales to more than justify sponsoring Mike's motocross racing?

**Taxpayer:** Not a problem. I have and will make a lot more than I am spending.

The taxpayer's entire cost of sponsoring Mike's motocross racing could be considered an ordinary and necessary business deduction. Ordinary and necessary are requirements of Code Section 162 to qualify as a business deduction. Sponsorship of racing is an ordinary event. Even the US Government sponsors motor sports racing teams. For example, Dale Earnhardt Jr. is sponsored by the National Guard. Naturally, marketing is considered a necessary business function.

Motocross, being a fun thing to do, requires special attention to the profit motivation. In this case the profit motivation exists and can be well documented. As a taxpayer would you rather deduct just the cost of the logos or your son's entire sponsorship cost?

# Vacation Your Way to Less Tax

Travel is a popular pastime enjoyed by most Americans. Unfortunately, since most travel is considered a personal expense, the tax code does not permit it to be a tax deduction. The strategy of deducting these costs lies in combining business with leisure travel.

Sadly, this strategy is not as easy as labeling your travel as business related; but if you plan your trips the right way, you can really stretch your tax dollar! The first landmine you must overcome is the primary purpose for the travel:

- Primarily vacation, with a little business mixed in = little or no deduction.
- Primarily business trip, with a little fun mixed in = mostly deductible.

Did your accountant forget to tell you how to structure your travel to qualify as business travel and withstand IRS scrutiny?

Did your accountant forget to tell you how to legitimately justify taking a spouse, partner, significant other, and possibly a child on a business trip?

Did your accountant forget to tell that you **don't** need to save receipts for business travel expense that are less than $75, except lodging? If they have, it may be time to work with someone new.

There is an old joke in the accounting profession:

How do you hire an accountant?

You ask each applicant, "What is 2 plus 2?" Some may say "4," but the first one to say "What do you want it to be?" is the guy you hire.

The truth behind the joke is that tax accounting is an art, not a science. You do not want to hire a person who gives you off-the-cuff answers. You want someone who is going to look high and low before giving you an answer you can use. The art of being a Certified Tax Coach is knowing what the taxpayer wants to achieve and coaching them safely, successfully,and legally through the landmines hidden in the tax law.

# Wrapping it up!

How did your current accountant do? Are there *"Things Your Accountant Forgot to Tell You"*? Could there be a lot more forgotten items?

Tax accountants are strong at recording your tax history. Certified Tax Coaches are strong at **writing your tax future!**

I am not telling you everything I know or everything you need to know. This is not a "How to Book." These concepts require professional tax help. As the Mythbusters would say, "Don't try this at home!"

For more information on choosing the right advisor for the job, read Chapter Thirteen in this book.

# Craig Hawkins, CPA CTC

Craig Hawkins, CPA and business coach with 27 years of experience working with countless small businesses. He has developed a unique ability to jump start businesses and increase business profits.

Craig is from Kennewick, Washington. He received a B.S. in Accounting from Brigham Young University in 1981 and earned his Certified Public Accountant License in 1984.

Craig started his own CPA business in Washington State in 1986. He has worked with start-up, micro and small businesses using his knowledge to help each one become more successful.

Craig decided to move his family to Florida in 2001 to be closer to his wife's family. He currently is practicing in Tampa, Florida while maintaining a number of clients in Washington State. Through Craig's 27 years of experience, he has been able to gain insights into the challenges and opportunities that face growing businesses.

Craig is a problem solver who opens the eyes of business owners to issues which they may not be aware of. Craig looks at the big picture when it comes to business, not just the issue at hand.

# CHAPTER THREE

# New Businesses 101: Tax Strategies for Freelancers and The Forced Entrepreneur

## By Eric Levenhagen, CPA CTC

Owning your own business can be both scary and rewarding at the same time. I have had the pleasure of working with a number of small business owners and freelancers in my business. Some of them have been their own bosses for years and others are just starting a new business for the first time. When I ask them what type of plan they have in place to manage their taxes, I usually get a blank stare.

Most people think they pay too much in taxes. The problem is they don't know what to do about them. I know business owners who will spend hours pouring over their Profit & Loss statements looking for ways to cut expenses or "trim fat." They are managing all of the expenses in their business except for one of the biggest annual expenses they have — taxes.

It is possible to manage your income taxes, as you have already learned in other parts of this book, by having a written plan. Usually I have found smaller business owners — those working out of their home or just getting started — have some mental roadblocks as to why a written tax plan will not work for them. They usually believe one of three myths:

- They cannot afford tax planning
- The IRS will come after them if they claim too many deductions
- They don't have the time to keep all the records the IRS requires

Let's take these myths and tear them apart right now. First of all, there is no such thing as a business too small to benefit from tax planning. Owning a business is *the* best tax shelter left in America. There are many more deductions and tax strategies available to a small business owner than there is to anybody else, period. The only trick is using your business as a vehicle to *maximize* your tax benefits.

Also included in the first myth is the thought you have to make a lot of money in your business to need tax planning. This couldn't be further from the truth. As we'll talk about later, you don't even necessarily need to show a profit in order to take advantage of these strategies. Again, the business itself is opening the door for you to take advantage of the savings built into the tax law. I often say it doesn't matter if you make $2,000 or $20,000,000 in your business; there are strategies out there to help you.

Many people believe they cannot afford tax planning. While good tax planning can be expensive, investing in tax planning pays big returns! As you've seen throughout this book, the right strategies can save you thousands each year. Given this thought, you can't afford NOT to do tax planning!

The second myth about fearing the IRS is just absurd. Would you be afraid of a police officer if you weren't breaking the law? If you saw a $20 bill on the ground that wasn't yours, and a police officer was standing right there, would you bend over and pick it up? Or would you leave it because you are afraid of what the officer would do or say? Picking up money off the ground is not illegal. As long as you aren't breaking the law there is no reason to fear the police.

The same holds true for the IRS. They are simply the law enforcement of taxes. As long as you aren't doing anything illegal you have nothing to worry about. And please do not mistake the strategies in this book for being "aggressive" or raising "red flags." All of the strategies here have been court-tested and IRS approved. They are all written in black and white right in the tax law. A good tax advisor will show you where in the law these strategies are written. This will ease your mind and will also start audit-proofing your return so if the IRS does review your taxes you will have nothing to worry about. There really is no sense in fearing the IRS.

The third and final myth is as much of an excuse as a myth. The myth portion of not having time to do some basic record keeping is that it really does not take much time as long as you have a system in place and know what to keep. Your accounting system is an important aspect of your business, no matter how big the business. Take some time to get it set up correctly at first, or find somebody to help you. But don't ignore it because you don't have the time. It's like anything else worthwhile. It will take some time and effort to get it going, but once it's there it will be a valuable tool for you to use in the longrun.

Now that we have removed these barriers, let's look at some actual strategies to help you realize all of these savings we are talking about. Some of them you may have heard of before, others may be completely new to you. But all of them probably have at least one component you didn't know about before.

## Preserve Business Losses

It is normal for a new business to show a loss the first couple of years, especially when taking into consideration all of the great strategies you are learning in this book. Some businesses can even show a loss for multiple years in a row. There is an old myth that your business has to show a profit every three years in order to be considered a business. This is not entirely true.

Actually, to be considered a business all you need is a profit <u>motive</u>. You need to have the intention to make a profit in a business-like fashion. As long as you do, it doesn't matter whether you actually make a profit or not, your venture is still considered a business.

What's the risk here? If you don't have a profit motive, you don't have a business. If you don't have a business, the IRS considers your venture a hobby. You don't want a hobby. You still have to claim all the income you make from your hobby. You might be able to deduct hobby expenses, if you can itemize deductions. But hobbies cannot report a loss. Only a business can record a loss on a tax return. The business loss offsets other income so it drives your taxes down. But if your business is classified as a hobby, you lose the ability to record losses and you lose the deduction!

So how do you document and prove your intent to make a profit? It's really quite easy, just run your business like an actual business. Have a business plan of some sort. It doesn't have to be long and fancy like what the bank wants to see for a loan application. Just have written goals about how you plan to sell your product or service, who you're going to sell to, and how you're going to deliver to your customers. You can include some simple financial projections as well to show how you would make a profit if you reached all of your sales goals. Then just make sure you are doing things to help you reach those goals. Print some business cards and brochures for your business, set up a website, and advertise, simple things that all businesses do anyway. As long as you prove you are actively trying to make a profit the IRS can't take away this deduction.

# Converting Personal Assets to Business Use

If you are a new business owner or are working from your home, there are usually some items you have taken from your personal belongings to use in your business instead of buying everything new. Even if you don't use these items 100% in your business, you may still be able to take a deduction for them.

Think about the things you use in your office. Your desk, chairs, furniture, computer, and cell phone are all possibilities. First you need to figure out how much the asset is worth today. A computer you purchased a year ago isn't worth as much today as you paid for it originally. So figure out how much it would be to replace that exact same computer today. The same goes for any other assets such as furniture.

If you use these assets 100% in your business, you can simply claim the replacement value you just came up with. Otherwise you have to document how often you use these assets for business use and come up with a business use percentage, or BUP. Let's say you log your cell phone use and 80% of the time you use it to make business calls. Let's also assume it would cost you $100 to replace your phone when you first started using it in your business. $100 times 80% would give you an $80 deduction. That may not sound like a lot, but it will add up quickly if you start counting everything else. Don't overlook this conversion to give your deductions an extra boost.

# Vehicle Deductions

If you drive your own car for business use, you can claim part of the cost as a deduction. Most people rely on the "standard mileage" method for claiming this deduction because they think it is easier. The IRS actually allows two methods of computing this deduction. The standard mileage method simply applies a standard rate to the number of miles you have driven for business. For the last six months of 2011, the rate is 55.5 cents per mile.

Do you think the cost of operating a small compact car is the same as an SUV? Of course it's not. So why settle for one standard rate to claim your deduction? In reality, most vehicles actually cost more to operate than what the IRS allows for the standard mileage rate. The good news is you can also use the "actual expenses" method to figure your deduction. This takes into account what you actually spend to operate your vehicle, like gas, maintenance, insurance, tires, oil changes, car washes, and parking costs. You can even deduct a portion of the interest on your car loan and depreciation if you own your car.

In order to do this, again you have to figure a business use percentage, or BUP, for your vehicle. You will have to keep track of all the miles you drive your vehicle in one of three categories: commuting, personal, and business.

Commuting miles are generally your first trip of the day to your first business stop, or a place where you conduct business. This could be your office or a customer's location. Your last trip of the day from your office to your home is also commuting miles.

Business miles can be counted when you start driving from one business location to another. If you drive from your office to a client's office, those are business miles. You can also count business miles when you drive from your office to do business tasks like go to the office supply store, the post office, or the bank.

Personal miles are anything in between not business related. If you go to the store and pick up a few household items over lunch it is a personal trip. Driving out of town on a personal vacation is also personal mileage.

Business miles are deductible, personal and commuting miles are not. Take your total business miles and divide by your total miles in all three categories to find your BUP. This is the percentage you can apply to all of your actual expenses for the deduction.

The more business miles you drive, the higher your BUP and the more actual expenses you can deduct. Now here's a cool way to combine a couple of strategies. The IRS says when we leave our home and go to our office it is a personal trip and does not count as business miles. But what if you could start every day at your office without driving? If you qualify to claim a home office, you can "commute" to your office every day without even leaving your home. Then, as long as you leave from your home office and drive to a business stop, this first actual driving trip of the day becomes deductible business mileage. Claiming the home office deduction allows you to boost the BUP for your vehicle deductions!

In order to track your business miles, keep a log of where you drive, its business purpose, and the number of miles for that trip. Notice that the record-keeping requirements, which were supposed to be easier for the standard mileage allowance, are close to the same under either method. Both methods require you to track your mileage the same way. Just set up a separate file for gas receipts and other actual expenses and you are set to use either method. Generally if you have a high BUP the actual expense method will result in a higher deduction. If you have already been using the standard mileage method, you can switch to the actual expense method as long as you own your car.

# Meals and Entertainment

This is an area a lot of people get into trouble. Not because it is a high-risk deduction, because they simply do not know how to document their meals and entertainment expenses.

Let's go over the rule first. You can deduct 50% of your meals and entertainment if they are related directly to your business or if you have a business discussion during, before, or after the event. You can deduct meals and entertainment with customers and clients, prospects, employees, and any other business contacts. If you provide a personal service, this can be almost anybody you eat with! Sometimes entertainment venues, such as a theater or sporting event, may not be a good place to hold a conversation. So the rule states the business discussion can take place directly before or after the event.

Now let's bulletproof this deduction. The IRS looks for five key pieces of evidence to allow meals and entertainment deductions. They want to know the cost, date, place, business purpose, and business relationship of your guest. Take a look at that list, then take a look at your day planner or calendar, then look at the list again.

Can you see most of the required information there already? I know when I make a lunch appointment I mark down the place and name of my guest on the date the meal will happen. I just add a little description of the business purpose and record the cost of the meal. So the next time you fill out your calendar for an appointment, get in the habit of making these extra notations. Instead of "lunch with John Smith at 12:00," write something like "Smokey's Bar & Grille with John Smith to discuss possible referrals."

Now we have four of the five pieces of key information right on our calendar. Remember to record the cost of the meal after it has happened and you are done with the record-keeping requirements. Another nice feature of this deduction is if you spend less than $75 at one establishment and keep the five pieces of information in your planner, you don't even need to keep the receipt!

One thing normally overlooked with this deduction is the cost of home entertainment. Do you ever host a dinner party and invite customers or prospects? If you are entertaining business-related individuals at your home, the cost of those meals are deductible too! And if you invite guests to a "dinner seminar" at your home, you could deduct 100% of the meal instead of the normal 50% deduction! This is because the meal becomes an integral part of your sales seminar.

Be sure to take pictures of your event and put them into your tax file along with the invitations you sent and a copy of any handouts provided. Anything to prove you had guests over for a business seminar. Otherwise the IRS may look to take this deduction away, saying you just had friends over for dinner.

The best feature about these strategies is I have not once told you to spend more money anywhere. Take a look at those strategies again. Every one of them deals with converting money you already spend into a tax deduction! So don't overlook these areas or discount them, these are truly powerful strategies. For more information on using your business as a great tax shelter, see Chapter Four. The key is to use your business as a vehicle to *maximize* your tax benefits. When you can do this, you'll turn these strategies into cash!

Want even more information on these tax planning strategies and more? Download bonus resources for this book at www.SecretsOfATaxFreeLife.com.

## Summary

- Don't overlook tax planning because you're afraid or don't think it applies; these are myths.
- Even if your business is not profitable you can still benefit from proper tax planning.
- Document your profit intent to protect your business loss deductions.
- Take deductions for personal property converted to business use.
- Keep a daily log of your vehicle mileage and classify as personal, commuting, or business.
- Save receipts for all actual expenses including gas, oil, and maintenance.
- Use your home office to boost your business mileage.

- Record the five key pieces of information in your day planner for meals and entertainment.
- For meals and entertainment, you don't need receipts for any single expense less than $75.
- Don't overlook home dinner parties as possible deductions.

**Want to learn more tax planning secrets?**

Bonus free resources are available
at www.SecretsOfATaxFreeLife.com.

# Eric Levenhagen, CPA CTC

1415 4th St. SW
Mason City, IA 50401

(641) 424-3990 Office
(888) 892-5132 Toll Free

Email: Eric@IowaTaxPlanner.com
www.IowaTaxPlanner.com

We are dedicated to exceeding our client's expectations by delivering exceptional, professional service with a personalized touch. Founded in 2005, ProWise Tax & Accounting specializes in proactive tax planning strategies for business owners, self-employed individuals, farmers, investors, and individuals.

Eric Levenhagen holds a bachelor's degree in accounting as well as a master's degree in accounting & financial management. He has worked as a staff accountant for a local CPA firm and has also served as controller of various closely held companies.

Eric is enthusiastic about the challenge of helping clients manage their personal and business financial matters. Eric is both a Certified Public Accountant and a Certified Tax Coach who integrates both disciplines into a holistic, client-centered approach towards maximizing his clients' after-tax income and wealth.

Eric trains hard so you can rest easy. In addition to the annual hours he spends maintaining his certifications, he spends hundreds of hours studying tax strategies and real world business challenges like marketing, management, operations, and human resources. He takes that knowledge, combines it with all of his experience, and customizes a plan just for you.

Outside of the office, Eric enjoys spending time with his wife and kids. His hobbies include reading, following college and professional football, and music. Finally, Eric is an aspiring traveler and hopes one day to be able to take his family many places around the world.

# CHAPTER FOUR

# The Last Legal Tax Shelter in America: Owning Your Own Business

## By Kim Bey, CPA CTC

The Great American Dream of owning your own business is still alive! Many Americans view entrepreneurship as a way to pursue the American Dream, take control of their lives and support their families. For many, owning a business is a part of the American Dream, and for others, this opportunity is driven by necessity, as rising unemployment rates are turning laid-off workers into entrepreneurs.

There are some 600,000 new businesses founded each year and many have experienced amazing results. Just look around and see new business ideas in your area, or read many success stories of young entrepreneurs on the internet. I often wished I was the one who came up with many of the ideas, some are absolutely brilliant, and some are so simple yet so powerful. It took someone with a vision and great execution to enjoy great success.

Entrepreneurs are those who create business and jobs. Most tax laws were written with the small business owners in mind; the best advantages available for legitimate tax exemptions reside with the business owners. Many tax laws are specifically related to and structured based on what structure is chosen for your small business. Even if you already have a business form or structure which is non-optimum tax-wise, as you've seen in Chapter Four, this can often be easily changed.

Most individuals overpay their taxes. Even most small businesses overpay on their taxes. Not knowing how specific tax laws related to your unique business circumstances can be expensive at best. A well planned, solid tax strategy tailored to your unique situation will help you shelter the maximum portion of your income from unnecessary taxes and be completely legal.

# Key Facts About The Tax System That Make Business Ownership Vital

### Ability To Spend Pre-Tax Dollars Instead Of After-Tax Dollars

You are going to spend your money on things you need or things you want. How you set up your business affects how you classify these expenses and has enormous tax consequences.

One of the key components to tax planning is the ability to shift after tax dollars into pre-tax dollars.

Tax deductions reduce your taxable income. If you're in the 15% tax bracket, an extra dollar of deductions cuts your tax by 15 cents. If you're in the 35% tax bracket, that same extra dollar of deductions cuts your tax by 35 cents.

When you are an employee, the government takes its share first; with each and every paycheck. Your ability to provide for your expenses rests in whatever amount is leftover. To lower your taxes, you can contribute to 401(k) plan, cafeteria plans or may be health savings account or some other retirement plan if you qualify. Owning a rental property might help, but there are not a lot of options available.

On the other hand, the real key to paying a lot less in tax is learning how to shift your after-tax dollars into pre-tax dollars. Owning a business provides a legal way to accomplish this. When set up correctly, a business pays its expenses first, and then the owner or owners pays tax on the amount leftover. By creating a business, you can control the amount of money you spend on taxes. This is how Warren Buffet and millions of other wealthy Americans pay less tax per year than an employee earning a $60,000 salary!

### Owning a Business Allows You to Take Advantage of Tax Credits.

Tax credits are dollar-for-dollar tax reductions, regardless of your tax bracket. So, if you're in the 15% tax bracket, a dollar's worth of tax credit cuts your tax by a full dollar. If you're in the 35% bracket, an extra dollar's worth of tax credit cuts your tax by the same dollar. There's no secret to tax credits, other than knowing what's out there.

Government is allowing more and more tax credits for businesses and you being in business for yourself allows you to take advantage of this.

### Choosing the Right Business Structure for Your Particular Circumstances Allows You to Minimize Your Taxes.

When you are in business for yourself, the business entity you establish determines how your profit from the business will be taxed. So choosing the business structure is essential.

## Business Structures

There are several types of entities possible. One has these basic choices:

### Sole proprietorship

This is the easiest of all the entities to establish and least expensive to operate from administrative standpoint. You will report your business income on Schedule C of your personal tax return. In addition to paying your federal and state income tax on the net profit of your business, you

**Three Basic Forms of Business:**

1. **Sole proprietorships** (businesses with one owner)

2. **Partnerships** (businesses with more than one owner)

3. **Corporations** (a separate legal entity governed by state law)

pay self-employment tax on that profit as you are now the employer and employee. The key to sole proprietorship tax savings is knowing what you can and cannot deduct as expenses.

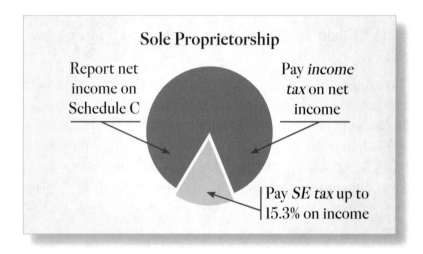

## Partnerships

Partnerships present some of the most complex areas of legal and tax law. Profit and losses are "pass through" to the individual partner's tax returns. In turn, the individual partners pay tax at whatever their personal tax rate. However, profits earned in a partnership are generally subject to self-employment tax, this sometimes can be more than the owner's federal income tax!

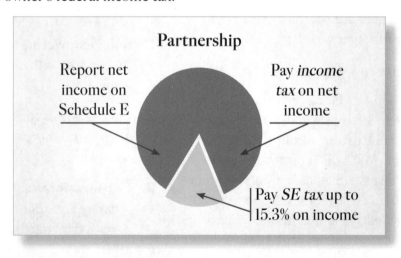

## S-Corporation

S-Corporation is another "pass-through entity" where net profits are passed through to the individual shareholders, who each pay taxes on their share at their own individual rates. The S-corporation pays you a reasonable wage for the work you do, and you pay the tax on that income on your own return. So the owners' income is split into two parts — wages and pass-through distributions from the S-Corporation. Distributions are not subject to self-employment tax and can create substantial savings for the owners.

Let's say your profit at the end of the year is $80,000. If you are operating as a sole proprietorship, you will pay $11,304 in self-employment tax (SE Tax) as your profit is subject to SE Tax. If you are operating as an S-Corporation and you pay yourself a salary of $40,000, and take the remaining profit as shareholder distributions, you would save $5,184 in SE Tax.

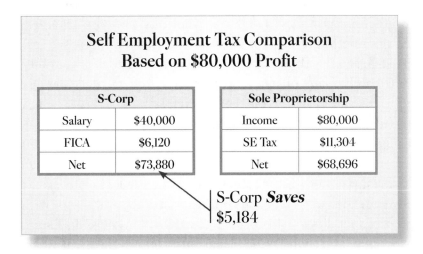

### Self Employment Tax Comparison
### Based on $80,000 Profit

| S-Corp | | Sole Proprietorship | |
|---|---|---|---|
| Salary | $40,000 | Income | $80,000 |
| FICA | $6,120 | SE Tax | $11,304 |
| Net | $73,880 | Net | $68,696 |

S-Corp **Saves** $5,184

## C Corporation

C Corporation is a separate legal entity governed by state laws, files its own tax returns and pay tax at special corporate tax rates. Sometimes tax rates can be lower than individual owner's tax rates. When profits are distributed to the shareholders in the form of dividends, the owners pay tax on their own individual rates — "double" tax on profits — first at the corporate level and then as the owners withdrew profits from the business. However, C Corporations usually have the most allowable deductions of any business structure, including the ability to deduct fringe benefits for the owners such as education assistance, Health and life insurance, company owned cars, etc.

## LLC

The LLC is a relatively recent type of business structure which offers a hybrid between a partnership and an S-corporation. Profits are paid on a pass-through basis to its individual owners. LLC is an extremely flexible entity structure which can be taxed in several ways – sole proprietorship, S-Corporation or C-Corporation.

### Choosing which entity structure works best for you.

How do you know what entity structure works best for you? Each type of entity structure provides its own sets of legal and tax advantages. There are times it may be highly beneficial tax-wise and for asset protection purposes to divide up your business into separate parts based on function or type of income, and then set up more than one entity structure for the different portions or functions of your business. Unfortunately many business owners approach the decision of which structure is right for them by consulting with an attorney whose recommendations usually focus mostly on the legal benefits and nuances surrounding the entity choice. A much better basis for this choice is based on tax benefits and liability protection.

Ask yourself, or better yet, ask your qualified Tax Advisor: "What kind of my expenses will various business structures allow me to deduct as pre-tax spending?" This breaks down into: "Where do I spend the most money" and then "Which legal entity allows the greatest amount of this to be a deductible expense?" There are other factors to consider, but being able to categorize expenses as deductible is in most cases the most important factor.

# Setting Up for the Future

No matter if you are starting up a new enterprise or already in business, deciding on the structure of your business can make huge differences in tax savings. The structure of your business may have been appropriate at the beginning of your business, but as your needs change with time, it may not be effective now for tax purposes. Ask yourself regularly: "What pre-tax spending will your business structure provide you, and is this the area which will benefit you most?" Look at your spending patterns, where you spend the most money. Does the business entity you are considering provide a tax advantage for this type of expense?

At the end of the day, if you are serious about keeping more of what you earn through proactive tax planning, you need an expert on your side. Nobody can be an expert at everything, and the tax code is complicated and changes. Enlisting the help of a tax planning specialist can help you find the best entity structure and save the most money. Modern technology provides many opportunities to work with the RIGHT advisor, even if that person is across the country, instead of across the street.

# Retroactive Tax Benefits

In some instances past tax filings can be amended to recover taxes previously paid.

# Real Life Examples of Tax Savings

1. An independent consultant who consistently earns over $300,000 per year in gross income and came to us for help to reduce her taxes. We recommended that she continues to operate as a sole proprietorship (because she lives in a state where S-Corporations must pay state corporation tax). We helped her set up a Medical Expense Reimbursement Plan (MERP) and retirement plan. As a result, she was able to pay her out of pocket medical expenses of more than $10,000 with pre-tax money and was able to contribute the maximum amount to her retirement account and reduced her taxes by approximately $24,000 yearly on an ongoing basis.

2. A new IT professional/web designer client came to us right before year end, he has a great start to his business and generated over $100,000 in revenue in his first year and earned over $4,000,000 in his third year. His previous CPA told him that there was not much they could do to reduce his taxes. He was set up as an LLC, but we helped him elect to be taxed as an S Corp and he now enjoys savings on self employment tax alone of more than $80,000 per year. Other tax savings included setting him up for maximum retirement contribution, and a Closely Held Insurance Company (CHIC) so that tax savings were even greater and will continue.

3. A young college student who does freelancing on a part time basis and was earning almost $100,000 per year. We helped him set up to be taxed as an S Corporation. In addition to his SE Tax savings of over $7,000 per year, he is able to deduct a portion of his rent, and some other operating expenses as business expenses. By setting up a Solo 401k plan, he additionally is able to contribute the maximum amount to his retirement plan to further reduce his taxes and as a result he is really getting off on the right foot in life financially.

# Owning Your Own Business

### Analyze Your Business Model.

How do you make sure you achieve the great American dream and not a great American nightmare? It is vital to have a business plan that includes cash flow projections as there are fixed costs associated with running a business regardless of the amount of revenue you create. At our firm, we provide a service called "Business Sanity Check" to help new business owners or someone considering starting a new business (or even an existing business considering a new product or market) analyze their business to determine if it is going to be viable and how long it will take, or are they going to end up with an "expensive hobby."

I met with three young entrepreneurs who were in the process of taking out a home equity loan to purchase a franchise and scheduled an appointment with me to help them set up an LLC. I advised them to run a business sanity check on their business model. We spent three hours working on their cash flow projections and they were shocked to learn that it would take them more than two years to reach break-even cash flow for that business model and they would have needed an additional half a million dollars plus to capitalize their business. I asked them if they had access to that kind of capital and all three of them shook their heads. They were disappointed but greatly relieved, as they had almost bought into an expensive hobby!

## Develop Both Defensive and Offensive Financial Strategies.

Tax planning, including getting the right structure and taking advantage of all decisions available, make up the most important part of your *defensive* financial strategy — defending the money you earn from unnecessary taxation. Equally important is the *offensive* strategy you adopt — how you will make the maximum money from your business. This includes the fact that the biggest "losses" a company typically experiences is the failure to take advantage of opportunity.

Peace of mind and prediction regarding taxes, accurate financial information with useful compilations and metrics, and counseling on marketing and other business strategies make it possible to find and actively pursue those highly profitable opportunities which are available for every business.

## Contribute To The Economy And The World Around You.

The small business engine is what is going to turn our economy around. According to the Small Business Administration (SBA), small firms were responsible for generating 64% of net new jobs over the past 15 years. We need brave, passionate entrepreneurs now more than ever. By following your passion and vision, you are not only embarking on an exciting journey, but you have the power to build opportunity for yourself and for others. Your small business can help put our country back to work.

## Satisfy Your Inner Purposes — The Biggest Satisfaction in Business Ownership.

One of my basic purposes is helping people and seeing them expand and do well in business and in life. Having my own business has allowed me to help many business owners expand their business, realize their dreams and win in life. One of my greatest joys is knowing that I have truly helped someone and this satisfaction is priceless.

From working with business owners over the years, I have observed that business owners achieved a lot of satisfaction from the following:

- Being their own boss and choosing who they want to work with
- Making more money and keeping more of what they earned than they would if they were working for someone else
- The enjoyment which comes from challenging themselves
- The self confidence derived from creating and running a successful business

# Summary

Business ownership and entrepreneurship gives you the opportunity to pursue your passions in life, and with effective and innovative tax planning the government will reward you handsomely for this with tax benefits which allow you to keep more of your hard-earned money.

# Kim Bey, CPA, CTC

President & CEO
Bey & Associates, CPA, PC

www.DCCPA.Pro

Kim Bey is the founder and President of Bey & Associates, CPA, PC., a Washington, DC based accounting firm specializing in helping professional service firms across the country minimize their taxes through proactive tax planning, consulting and ongoing maintenance/back office support. Kim is Washington, DC's first Certified Tax Coach and a member of an elite group of fewer than 200 accountants nationwide that are dedicated to tax planning to save clients' money. She is an author and public speaker. She was featured in Washington Post as *the* expert in "Filing Taxes" article in 2009, Washington City Paper — DC's finest 2010, and a workshop speaker at Digital Capital Week (DC Week) in 2011.

A CPA since 1990, Kim has worked as staff accountant, senior examiner, auditor, audit & compliance manager at various organizations including a government agency and a National CPA firm where she gained the experience of working with a wide diversity of clients, large and small. In 2008, Kim founded Bey & Associates, CPA with 4 primary objectives:

- Helping wonderful clients keep more of their hard earned cash.
- Taking the dread and stress out of money matters such as taxes, accounting, cash flow uncertainties, etc.
- Providing practical effective money management counseling as a routine part of tax and accounting services to clients.
- Giving clients financial prediction in their businesses by giving them the tools necessary to create reserves, make more profits and expand while remaining viable and thus achieve personal peace of mind.

As a seasoned professional, Kim continuously focuses attention to saving tax money for her clients. She keeps abreast of the latest changes in tax codes, typically resulting in savings of hundreds or thousands of dollars in taxes which are often missed by other tax professionals.

Kim is licensed as a Certified Public Accountant in Washington, DC and Virginia. She earned her BBA degree in Accounting from the University of Oklahoma and completed several graduate courses, including Advance Income Tax Research and Business Finance at the University of Texas in Dallas.

She is an active community member in the Greater Washington, DC area and volunteers for various social betterment programs. Kim enjoys life through ballroom dancing, traveling, raising her 2 children and many outdoor activities.

If you are wondering if you pay too much tax, visit www.DCTaxCoach.com and download our FREE report "10 Most Expensive Tax Mistakes That Cost You Thousands."

# CHAPTER FIVE

# The Secrets to a Tax Free Life with Real Estate Investment

## By Larry Stone, CPA CTC

My interest in real estate investment comes naturally. I inherited it from my father and grandfather. Both were farmers who lived off the proceeds of their land. In addition, my uncles invested in their own real estate activities. So, I come from a family of real estate investors.

In addition to the farm, my father owned multiple properties. He rented these properties in order to supplement his cash flow and increase his wealth. My father used the "bootstrap" method of investing. He would purchase a property and live in it. Later, he would build another residence and rent out the previous home. Real estate investing has been in my family for years. I recall my father continuously planning alternatives to take advantage of the tax laws in order to keep the most cash possible for his family and his investments. It takes a plan to succeed in real estate investing.

Following my father's tradition, I have successfully owned real estate investments and I am currently managing multiple rental properties both residential and commercial. Using my father's example, I continually plan to improve the properties I manage. Many planning opportunities exist with real estate investment to build your wealth and reduce your taxes while saving your cash for your own investment purposes.

From the beginning of our country's history, real estate has been one of the keys to gaining wealth. Our founding fathers were landowners and real estate investors. Many of them received fees for services rendered and made payments for services received with their real estate investments during difficult times.

Under our current tax system, real estate provides one way to grow wealth while reducing your income tax liability. As your equity increases, the taxes are deferred until you sell the property and recognize the profit related to ownership. With careful planning, you may use strategies to defer your taxes to future years or exclude paying them altogether. It is one of the secrets to a tax free life.

Building equity in your real estate is simply a function of correctly selecting properties which will appreciate in value and taking advantage of the loan amortization schedule. Real estate values are locally determined. The phrase used by many realtors is true. Location, location and location are the three most important considerations when purchasing property. Another version of this saying is to buy the least expensive property in the most expensive neighborhood you can afford. You must carefully research any property purchase and thoroughly understand the characteristics of any potential acquisition. You should consider zoning, demographics, neighborhood, income levels and rental trends for any potential factor which would cause the purchased property to increase in value over time.

As your equity increases in the property, you may not have to pay any taxes on the increase in your wealth when you carefully plan your investment. The preferred plan is to have sufficient cash generated to pay all expenses and still take advantage of the non-cash deductions allowed by the IRS code to defer your taxes into the future.

So, why is real estate a good investment?
- You control your investment
- You do not pay any intermediaries or middle men
- It is a hard asset and the current price of real estate is at a historical low

- You have a leveraged transaction and should take advantage of borrowed money
- You reduce your taxes with non-cash depreciation deductions
- You defer taxes on increases in equity as long as you choose
- Strategies exist to permanently exclude your gain in your property[1]

# Is this the right time to invest in real estate?

Now is a great time to invest in long term real estate investments because of the following conditions:

- Housing prices are lower
- Mortgage rates are historically low
- Lower prices for houses and lower mortgage rates increases cash generated by a rental property
- Rents are climbing in many areas due to increased demand
- Younger individuals are not comfortable with property investments due to the recent market crash and are more likely to rent

Yes. All the above factors create a positive environment to enter the real estate investment field. As more people avoid real estate investing and the cost of obtaining and financing properties are historically low, this is probably the best time to get in the real estate market with an income producing property.[2]

# Real estate rental income is passive

Real estate rental is presumed as a "passive activity" under Internal Revenue Code (IRC) 469. This means that you cannot use your passive losses to offset ordinary income. When passive losses exceed passive gains, they are suspended until sufficient passive gains arise for future offset or the entire activity is disposed.

---

1   SmartMoney.com, *Finally, Time to Buy a House*, October 14, 2011, author Jack Hough

2   WSJ.com, *Big Money Gets Into the Landlord Game*, August 2011.

Given these limitations, the secret is to invest with income producing long term rental opportunities which meet the exceptions from this presumption:

- Where the average rental period is 7 days or less such as lodging operations
- When significant services are provided by the owner and there is less than 30 days of rental use per occupant
- When extraordinary services are provided by the owner
- When the rental of the property is related to a non-rental activity (self-rent your property to your business)
- When the property is available for nonexclusive use by customers during defined business hours
- When the property is used by a business activity which the taxpayer owns by a partnership, S corporation or joint venture

Careful planning of your rental project may allow you to use the above exceptions to your advantage and allow you to avoid the passive presumption. When you qualify under these exceptions, your rental property may be used to offset ordinary income.

# Other secrets for real estate rentals treated other than passive

Two other strategies are used to overcome the passive activity presumption under IRC 469. The first is the active management of the property and the other is the real estate professional classification.

### Be an active manager of your property

If your Adjusted Gross Income (AGI) is $150,000 or less, you can claim up to $25,000 in rental real estate loss allowance from property you actively participate in managing. You have to own greater than 10% of the value of the activity or not participate as a limited partner. Active participation requires regular, continuous or substantial involvement. You can also qualify when your involvement is limited to making management decisions and hiring independent contractors to provide actual services.

When your real estate investment plan allows for a rental loss within the $25,000 limit and your AGI is within the limit, you would want to take advantage of this strategy.

If your income is too high to claim the rental real estate loss allowance, you can buy passive income generators such as oil and gas, equipment leasing or real estate limited partnerships for tax-free income to be "soaked up" by the real estate losses.

## Be a material participating real estate professional

The active real estate investor strategy may not fit everyone. What if you have greater than $25,000 loss in rental property due to multiple properties or your AGI is greater than $150,000? Assuming that you spend more than 750 hours annually taking care of property, and those hours are more than 50% of the time you spend working for a living, you may be materially participating in real estate and qualify as a "real estate professional." This strategy allows you to deduct your full loss from those activities regardless of your overall adjusted gross income.

You must meet the "material participation" test for the activity by participating throughout the year on a regular, continuous and substantial basis. To meet this standard, you must demonstrate participation in one of the following seven ways:

- You participate for more than 500 hours
- You provide "substantially all" management services
- You participate for more than 100 hours during the tax year and no one contributes more than you
- You "significantly participate" and your aggregate participation in all activities exceeds 500 hours
- You materially participate for any five tax years (not necessarily consecutive) during the ten tax years preceding the current one
- You materially participate by performing personal service activity for any three tax years preceding the current tax year
- You participate on a regular, continuous and substantial basis

Once you meet the material participation qualification above, you still must qualify as a real estate professional by meeting the following two further tests:

- You spend 750 hours per year in "real property trade or businesses" in which you materially participate
- You spend more than half your time working on real estate activities in which you materially participate

Qualifying real estate trades or businesses include property development, redevelopment, construction, reconstruction, acquisition, conversion, rental, operation, management or leasing or brokerage trade or business. Services performed as an employee do not count toward this requirement unless you own greater than 5% or more of the employer entity.

Although your material participation is defined separately for each rental activity, you can elect to treat all your real estate activities as a single activity. This election makes sense when no single activity will meet the 750 hour test alone to qualify as a real estate professional or you do not meet material participation status in every activity. You must make this election by filing a statement with your original tax return for any taxable year in which you qualify. The election is binding for the year made and all future years (even if you no longer qualify to make the election). You may only revoke the election when a "material change" in your facts and circumstances occurs.

You must keep a good business diary or appointment book to verify your hours of service.

## Secrets to maximize your deductible expenses with income producing rental property

Under IRC 212, you are allowed to deduct an expense if it has been paid or incurred for the production or collection of income or the management, conservation or maintenance of property held for income and it is an ordinary and necessary expense. With real estate investments in rental properties, you may deduct the following typical expenses in a pre-tax rather than an after-tax basis:

- **Mortgage interest** – This represents the cost of money used to purchase your investment plus the financing charges for any additions, improvements or equipment.

- **Local and long distance travel** – Any travel related to your real estate investment will be deducted as long as it is ordinary and necessary in purpose.
- **Actual vehicle cost or standard mileage rate** – This represents the cost to operate your vehicle for working on the rental property.
- **Overnight stays** – You may stay overnight when traveling to inspect your property or to perform other management activities.
- **Meals and entertainment** – Yes, you may deduct ordinary and necessary expenses with leads, prospects, tenants, referral sources and vendors. You should document who, when, where and what amount was spent. Keep your receipts for any amount expensed over $75.
- **Lodging** – Lodging may be necessary when you are working on the unit. All lodging receipts should be kept.
- **Home office** – You may require a home office to administer your real estate investment and to manage your property.
- **Hiring your family to perform tasks** – Your children or spouse may become employees or independent contractors to work on your property.
- **Cost to insure liability, casualty, and health** – Your real estate investment should insure for all the usual insurance requirements including medical expenses for employees.
- **Funding your child's education** – Plans exist to pay your child for work performed and to save those dollars to pay for their college education.
- **Legal and professional services** – You may deduct the cost of legal and professional expenses such as tax advice from your real estate investment.

Any time you can take an expense as a pre-tax rather than an after-tax deduction, you win. Naturally, you want to properly report the largest amount of expenses possible to your rental activity in order to take advantage of strategies to offset your ordinary income.

# Secrets to maximize the repair expenses made on your property

You can save thousands in tax simply by distinguishing repairs (deductible now) from improvements (deductible over time) under IRC 162 and 263. Repairs and maintenance keep your property in good operating condition. Consider expenses for things like painting, repairing broken windows, and fixing gutters, floors and leaks. You usually benefit by having deductible repairs over depreciable improvements.

Improvements will add value to your property, increase its useful life, or adapt it to a new purpose. These examples are room additions, upgraded appliances and fixtures, landscaping and replacement windows and roofs.

You should carefully determine and track repairs versus improvements. Request separate bills for separate jobs in regards to these classifications. Have contractors describe their work as repairs as appropriate rather than renovations or improvements. Use similar material when performing the work.

By carefully documenting your repairs, you will save thousands over time unless your losses are limited by passive activity rules.

# Secrets to making the most of your depreciation deductions on your property

With rental investments, you are allowed to deduct the depreciating value of the rental property over time under IRC 168. This depreciating value is not assigned to the raw land but on improvements, building structure and components. Unless you are limited by the passive activity rules, it is to your benefit to maximize this depreciation deduction as much as possible.

First, you must determine your basis. Your basis is generally the price you pay for the property. Divide the basis on your property between raw land and improvements. Assign as much value as possible to improvements. The IRS recommends using your local property tax assessment but you can use your own appraisal or insurer's estimate.

Assign as much value as possible to land improvements. Land improvements are depreciated over 15-year period.

Then, determine the remaining improvements between structure and personal property. Personal property items are appliances, cabinets, countertops, and carpeting. Assign as much value as possible to personal property because it depreciates over a 5-year life.

The remaining basis to allocate will be assigned to structural components such as roofs, windows, plumbing and other structural items. These components are depreciated over 27.5 years for residential properties and 39 years for commercial properties.

Most likely you will benefit by assigning the most value to the property class with the shortest life. This strategy allows you to use the non-cash depreciation deduction earlier.

# Other secrets to live a tax free life with real estate investing

Many secrets to a tax free life exist when investing with income producing real estate rental properties. Other secrets exist which you may prefer to use in excluding income from taxes.

### The secret of the serial personal residence exclusion

Rental real estate operations are not the only way to take advantage of the tax code with real estate investments. For selected qualified individuals with building and remodeling experience, you may use a personal residence strategy to permanently exclude gain from your taxable income.

Most people are aware that you can exclude $500,000 gain (married couple filing together) or $250,000 gain (single person) when you sell your personal residence under IRC 121. This exclusion is available every two years.

You are required to personally reside on the premises to establish your personal residence. If you purchase a house which requires significant remodel (upgrades to the building) or building a house on a vacant lot, you may place a mobile home on the lot to establish your residence. This would begin the calendar establishing your claim as a personal residence.

As you live on the premises, you perform the remodel or build the house. Let's assume you bought the vacant lot for $50,000. You build a 2,000 square foot single family house at approximately $100 per square foot or a total of $200,000. You would have a basis in your personal residence of $250,000.

After occupying the premises for two years, you decide to sell your personal residence. With a market value of $450,000, you would realize a $200,000 profit on the sale. Using the sale of personal residence exclusion, you would exclude this $200,000 profit from your income. You never have to pay the taxes on the $200,000 cash you keep. This strategy may be repeated every two years. Obviously, this is another secret of living a tax free life. This strategy works best for the individual who is skilled in remodeling or contracting a personal residence. It does take a plan to succeed in this opportunity to save your money.

## Secrets for the "fix and flip" real estate investor

For many, this strategy has been a successful investment strategy. If you buy property with the intent to resell "in the ordinary course of your trade or business," you are considered a dealer not an investor under IRC 1221. As a dealer, you are not eligible for most of the tax breaks that make real estate so attractive.

Unfortunately, there is no specific rule to determine if you qualify as a dealer or investor. The factors to consider are:

- What was your intent in buying the property – (Did you plan to sell it?)
- The length of your holding period – (Two years or less appears to reflect a dealer's intent)
- The number of transactions you have – (More sales in a year rather than 1 or 2 reflect a dealer's intent)
- The amount of income coming from the sale of the property – (Larger income from a property rather than smaller income from many properties reflect an investor intent)

- How active are you in selling the property – (Buying and selling fulltime, keeping a sales office, regularly advertising, and managing a sales staff indicate a dealer intent)

The IRS will consider these factors to determine whether you are a dealer or investor. Equal weight is not necessarily given to the above factors.

What is a dealer? A dealer earns ordinary income for the business and trade activities they perform. The property is treated similar to inventory. Gains are taxed as ordinary income rather than capital gains. Income earned is taxable by social security. You do not get to depreciate your property or use IRC 1031 like kind exchange to trade your property.

So, you routinely fix and flip properties but want to invest with rental property. You should consider the following secrets to reduce your pain:

- Separate your dealer properties from investment properties by holding them in distinct entities
- Avoid land and other complete contracts which cause entire gain as taxable when sale closes
- Consider selling property using lease options
- Take advantage of retirement plans, medical reimbursement plans and other employee benefits for active trade or business income

We do not know if real estate prices will increase, decrease or remain flat. "Fix and Flip" real estate activities work best when prices are rising. As a result, the dealer can plan to sell the property for more than they originally purchased it. Prior to purchasing a "Fix and Flip" property, you should calculate the Average Remodel Value (ARV) you expect to achieve and determine if this is achievable with your ability to perform the necessary repairs. This activity works best when you are able to obtain the property at a cost advantage in the first place such as an estate sale, tax lien, short sale or foreclosure.

If you are entering the "Fix and Flip" market without a history of dealer activity, one strategy that exists is to document that you plan to hold the property as an investment or rental. I would even suggest placing it on the rental market and advertise it for rent as soon as possible. This would provide you with a workable exit strategy should the "Fix and Flip" not proceed as anticipated. Without a track record, the decision to invest or deal is yours to write.

If your intent is strictly "fix and flip" you would qualify for dealer status and these transactions would result in ordinary income which is reported in the year earned rather than deferred. This is the disadvantage for this strategy.

# What is required to succeed with real estate investing?

Planning is required. It is true that some have been successful with real estate investments without a written plan. For the greatest success you must implement the plan and measure the return you get from the plan.

A written plan documenting the cash flow is necessary to identify the direction you are taking your project. In addition, a written plan will assist you in obtaining loans, making decisions and planning your tax strategy. Your plan should include strategies for exiting your investment.

You must carefully research and understand all decisions. The cheapest solution is not always the best solution. Any property purchases should be completely researched and the underlying values must be understood. You must be aggressive in managing the property and making decisions to minimize your largest cash expenses such as interest and property taxes.

Most important, you should have a personalized detailed strategic tax plan which identifies all the relevant tax strategies which you may use to reduce your taxes. But just don't work with any tax professional. Ask them how they invest their money. Tax professionals who invest in real estate activities will naturally follow real estate issues more closely than those who do not. They will be more in tune to your needs.

When you invest in real estate, you should carefully analyze the market and project. Then, you should develop your plan. With a full and complete understanding of the market where you plan to invest, and a carefully designed investment plan, you will increase your opportunities to succeed. Your planning should include selected strategies designed to reduce your taxes and keep your cash to reinvest. I encourage you to work with a tax professional that is both an experienced real estate investor and experienced in developing comprehensive tax reduction strategies.

Above all, take advantage of the secrets which exist with real estate investment to have a tax free life. The more money you keep in your pocket the less you have to earn.

# Larry D. Stone, CPA CTC

After graduating from Arizona State University with an MBA and acquiring his CPA, Mr. Stone spent the first 10 years of his career in the corporate world working for Phelps Dodge, General Dynamics and Martin Marietta. This involved auditing and compliance and then shifted to business planning and development. In 1996 he opened his CPA business specializing in the construction and real estate industry in the mountain resort town of Frisco, Colorado.

Larry is member and actively participates in the local builders association. This activity has developed into participation on the state and national level as well. As a result, he has many clients who are professional developers, general contractors, and others in the building trades.

Larry's interest and experience with real estate investing is one which he shares with many of his clients. They are attracted to his knowledge and expertise in this form of investing. A number of his clients invest in numerous real estate activities such as holding non-income producing property, managing residential and commercial real estate, and owning income producing investments. Other clients invest in trust deeds and tax liens. This variety provides him with a broad appreciation and in depth understanding of real estate investing.

Within Colorado, Larry provides education programs and seminars for real estate investor associations, giving their members information on how to take advantage of the tax code. In exchange, he learns many investing concepts in the real estate industry. Larry participates in both the contracting industry and real estate investment community. As a CPA tax professional, he has specialized training and experience in strategically reducing taxes and saving his clients their hard earned cash. As a result, he has earned the designation of "Certified Tax Coach." His firm specializes in identifying tax reduction opportunities, assisting clients with implementing their plan and then measuring the cash savings realized.

Regardless of where Larry's clients are located in the United States, they are just a touch away from his website, www.coloradotaxcoach. com, and a secure site for transmitting tax and financial information.

# CHAPTER SIX

# To LLC or Not to LLC — That is the Question

BY RONALD A. MERMER, CPA, CTC, CCPS

When deciding to go into business, whether it's for a business you are actively involved in on a day-to-day basis, or for an activity you passively invest in to create profits, one of the most common questions that comes up is "what type of entity should I set up?"

The most common forms to choose from include:

1. Sole Proprietor
2. Corporations – both C Corporations and S Corporations
3. LLCs, or Limited Liability Companies
4. Limited Partnerships

Each entity has its advantages and disadvantages. I will discuss the issues surrounding each type of entity (see the following entity comparison chart):

| COMPARISON OF ENTITIES | | | | |
|---|---|---|---|---|
| Type of Entities | Limited Liability | How Taxed | Subject to Self Employment Tax? | Fringe Benefits |
| Sole Proprietor | No | Individual | Yes | Limited |
| S Corp | Yes | Individual | On Payroll | Limited |
| C Corp | Yes | Corp & Individual | On Payroll | Yes |
| LLC | Yes | Individual or Corp. | Depends on how taxed | May be Limited |
| Limited Partnership | *Yes | Partnership | None for Limited Partner | Limited |

*Limited Partner*

**Sole Proprietorships,** most commonly referred to as a Schedule C or Self Employed Individual, is the least expensive way to start up a business. There is generally a fee paid to the local jurisdiction to file for a "DBA," which stands for Doing Business As. This is also one of the most costly ways when the business is profitable. All earnings are subject to FICA Tax on the full profit, currently limited up to $106,800 (increased to $110,100 for 2012), and Medicare Tax. Additionally, a sole proprietorship offers no personal liability protection. This would put all personal assets at risk. On the positive side, a sole proprietor offers the following benefits:

1. Hiring of children (if under 18, no payroll tax and the child then can fund a Roth IRA)
2. Hiring of a spouse which allows certain tax benefits
3. Medical expense reimbursement plans
4. Retirement savings
5. Education expense reimbursement

**C Corporations** are set up when an individual files incorporation papers with the State in which they conduct business. C Corporations offer liability protection from the shareholder's personal assets and offer several tax benefits. These benefits include, but are not limited to:

1. Medical expense reimbursement plan

2. Retirement benefits
3. Education expense reimbursement
4. Taxation of dividends at reduced rate (set to expire at the end of 2012)
5. Lower tax rate on the first $50,000 of taxable income

On the negative side, C Corporations have what is referred to as 'Double Taxation'. The corporation pays tax at the corporate level on its earnings and then the shareholder pays tax on the individual level when the money is paid out. This creates the 'double tax' issue. Additionally, the IRS can question both the reasonableness of salary as well as the accumulation of earnings within the corporation.

Both of these issues can result in additional tax. For example, if the Internal Revenue Service determines that the officer's compensation in a C Corporation is too excessive, the excess can be disallowed which could result in additional corporation tax. C corporations are also subject to a special tax called the accumulated earnings tax. If the Internal Revenue Service determines that the corporation is retaining too much of its profits, they must pay the extra tax on the excess profits. Additionally, having appreciated assets within a C Corporation can create a huge tax issue when selling the assets of the business because the corporation must pay tax on the profit from the sale of these assets, and then tax is paid again when the shareholder receives the profits from the corporation.

If the entity is a Personal Service Corporation (Accountants, Doctors, Lawyers and other licensed professionals), the corporate tax is computed at a flat rate of 35% of taxable income. You can see why C corporations have major tax disadvantages!

Although a C Corporation offers most fringe benefits as a tax deduction, the issues concerning the additional taxes should be weighed to determine whether this entity will provide the most tax advantages to its owners.

**S Corporation** refers to a corporation that has filed an election to be taxed as what is known as a pass-through entity. Pass through entities are those businesses whose profits "pass through" to the individual owners. The owner then pays tax on those profits based on whatever their individual tax rate is. An S Corporation is the most popular entity for most small business with limited shareholders. It offers ease of setup and taxation and also provides some degree of flexibility for its owners. The S Corporation offers the following benefits:

1. Amounts paid as distributions to shareholders are not subject to self-employment tax.
2. No Double Taxation issues
3. Retirement benefits
4. Liability protection on personal assets
5. No accumulated earnings tax concerns

On the other hand, the S Corporation has the following disadvantages:

1. Active shareholders must take a reasonable salary
2. Fringe benefits for shareholders who own greater than 2% of the stock of the corporation are not deductible.
3. Distributions made to shareholders must be in proportion to ownership percentage.
4. There is a limit to the number of shareholders that an S Corp can have.
5. Certain taxpayers and entities cannot be shareholders of an S Corporation.  S Corporations can be used to create tax savings which can be achieved at any income level.

I worked recently with a business owner client who was operating as a Sole Proprietorship. The business had one employee, and a net profit of $100,000. I advised him early in the year that he should incorporate and elect Subchapter S Status. By doing this, the business owner saved approximately $7,650 each year in tax just by making this one simple change.

Wondering how it works? Let me illustrate:

|  | Sole Proprietor | Subchapter S Corp |
|---|---|---|
| Net Income | $100,000 | $100,000 |
| *Reasonable Salary | $— | $50,000 |
| Income subject to self employment tax | $100,000 | $50,000 |
| Self employment tax rate | 15.3% | 15.3% |
| Self employment tax | $15,300 | $7,650 |
| **Total Tax Savings Each Year** |  | **$7,650** |

*Reasonable salary based on a comparative salary for a non-owner.*

This savings is not a one-time event. Rather, the business owner continues to keep over $7,000 of his hard earned money year after year! While the actual savings will be somewhat less due to fees related to the new corporation, this business owner was happy he could use tax planning to hang on to more of what he earns.

**LLCs, or, Limited Liability Companies,** offer the personal liability protection benefits as well as flexibility with tax treatment. While most LLCs are taxed as a partnership, the business has a choice and can make an election to be taxed exactly the same as a corporation. The LLC also enjoys other benefits as follows:

1. Personal asset protection
2. Flexibility with distributions to members
3. Retirement benefits
4. Increase in tax basis by guaranteeing debt – this is a great benefit for real estate investors
5. Pass-through taxation, similar to S Corporations
6. Flexibility with management issues
7. No ownership restrictions
8. Education expense reimbursement

On the negative side, the LLC has similar issues as the S Corporation does when it comes to fringe benefits. Certain fringe benefits paid for partners, or members owning greater than 2% are not deductible for tax. Another major disadvantage of LLCs taxed like partnerships is that the entire profit of the business is generally subject to self employment tax. The LLC can be an attractive choice for owners of real estate as it can offer both liability protection and some tax benefits.

# Limited Liability Companies

## Types of LLCs:

- Single member limited liability companies
- Limited Liability Companies filing as a corporation or partnership
- Series Limited Liability Companies
- Professional Limited Liability Companies

A **Single Member Limited Liability Company** can be treated as either a corporation or a disregarded entity. An election must be made to be taxed as a corporation. If no election is made, the single-member LLC will be taxed as a sole proprietorship. This means that all the tax disadvantages that apply to the sole proprietorship will apply to a single-member LLC.

A **Limited Liability Company** can also be treated as either a partnership or corporation by filing Form 8832. In order to be treated as a partnership, there must be more than one owner. If the business features multiple owners and no election is made, the entity will be taxed as a partnership.

A **Series Limited Liability Company** is a relatively new type of Limited Liability Company. This entity type provides asset protection across multiple series. Each individual series is protected against the other. Not all states recognize the Series LLC. Series LLCs are taxed under state laws which differ from state to state. This type of LLC is great for owning multiple real estate properties, all under one series, each being protected from liability issues of the others.

A **Professional Limited Liability Company** is an entity set up for businesses offering professional services and is formed under state law. This LLC usually is required for Doctors, Attorneys, Certified Public Accountants, Engineers and other licensed professionals.

Proper planning is essential to legally reduce income tax. Poor planning can result in thousands of wasted dollars as you can see in the following story I'd like to share with you.

I recently met with a new investor who owned several real estate rentals. He was qualified as a real estate professional which allowed him to deduct all of his losses on his rental properties. While reviewing his prior tax returns, I noticed that there was bank debt and no tax basis (a special requirement in tax law which allows investors to deduct losses). The investor was shocked when I told him the losses were not deductible since the properties were held in an S Corporation and there was no tax basis to take the loss.

If only he came to me prior to purchasing these properties. I would have advised him to set up LLCs, one for each property. By doing so, the bank debt which was personally guaranteed would have provided tax basis and the total loss would have been deductible. This error cost the taxpayer well over $25,000 in taxes that could have been invested and making him money. This lost opportunity shows why you need proactive tax planning to be successful. How much is the lack of tax planning costing you?

**Limited Partnerships** are entities created under State Law. A Limited Partnership consists of a General Partner and at least one limited partner. Limited Partnerships were popular prior to the establishment of Limited Liability Companies. Generally, a Limited Partnership is used for investors in real estate ventures. The Limited Partners have passive income and limited liability. The General Partner, has the liability associated with being a General Partner. For this reason, a Corporation is generally used as the general partner so that the shareholders are protected against any personal liabilities. A Limited Partnership is a good way to create passive income since a Limited Partner is considered not to be an active owner. Careful planning with different income streams can generate passive income which can be used to offset passive losses.

As you can see there are several choices when selecting the proper business entity, each with its advantages and disadvantages. It is important to consider each option, but everyone's individual situation is different.

One would need to look at the potential tax benefits, savings, and restrictions in order to decide which business structure will provide the most opportunities for the owner.

Ask yourself *why* you have selected the entity you use to hold your business and investments. If you don't know the answer, chances are you made the wrong choice. That choice can be costing you thousands of wasted tax each year. The good news is, it is never too late to make a change. Working with a good proactive tax advisor is essential to developing a plan that takes advantage of all the tax benefits business entities have to offer. Get started now to keep more of what you earn!

# Ronald A. Mermer, CPA, CTC, CCPS

Ronald A. Mermer has been practicing accounting and tax for over 30 years. His offices are located in the scenic lower Hudson Valley Region of New York State. Ron's approach to tax planning is to create a plan to help save his clients more money. Ron does this through proactive tax and financial planning. Ronald was honored as one of the select "2011 Hudson Valley Wealth Managers" by Hudson Valley Magazine. In addition to being a trusted business advisor, Ron is licensed as a Certified Public Accountant in New York and Florida, and is a Certified Tax Coach as well as a Certified College Planning Specialist.

Ron can be reached at:

Ron@mermcpas.com

www.mermcpas.com

# CHAPTER SEVEN

# Is Your 401K Plotting Against You?

## BY CRAIG E. WALDRON, EA CTC

You have put money into your 401K or other retirement type account. Is your 401K plotting against you? It is highly possible. Why?

The information contained in this chapter is meant to give potential and existing retirement account participants a fairly broad picture of retirement accounts and identify some of the major problems you can experience with them. I have not addressed every exception as a separate, rather lengthy book would be required to address each and every exception or variation of retirement account transactions.

In order to fully know what would apply in your particular situation, please consult a tax planning professional and preferably a Certified Tax Coach[1] who is trained to proactively plan to help you reduce tax.

---

1   Certified Tax Coaches are a leading group of tax professionals who are specially trained in the art of long term, proactive tax planning. In addition to their standard certifications and tax degrees, Certified Tax Coaches are required to complete comprehensive education focusing on high-impact tax planning strategies. Certified Tax Coaches are also required to adhere to the American Institute of Certified Tax Coaches Code of Ethics which provides assurance that the strategies

In addition to identifying some of the problem areas with retirement plans, a few examples of real life scenarios related to these issues are illustrated. I have also provided you with a series of questions you can use to evaluate whether or not a 401K or any other retirement plan may be the best option for you. Lastly, I have included a Q&A section with some of the most commonly asked questions I receive as a proactive tax advisor and Certified Tax Coach.

# The Problem Areas

First, let's start by identifying some of the common problems you may encounter when dealing with a retirement plan:

1.  Not knowing all of the rules for taking the money out may cause you to pay unnecessary penalties for withdrawing money too soon or too late
2.  Loss of control of your money
3.  Paying a higher percentage of taxes on the monies when you take them out than the percentage of taxes saved on money when it was put into the 401K
4.  Inherited retirement plans - Heirs or beneficiaries not knowing the following about money taken out of the plan:
    a.  How to pay the least amount of tax on it
    b.  What options they have
    c.  Or even that the money is taxable

Let's examine each of these areas in greater detail.

## 1.  Not knowing the rules for taking the money out.

When taken out too soon, you pay your current income tax rate which may be higher than the tax rate you were paying when you put the money in. Plus, you will pay a 10% penalty on top of that. If you take the money out too late, you still pay income tax on it, and, in addition, you'll pay a 50% penalty on what you should have taken out. The 50%

---

and ideas used to create your plan stay within the boundaries of the law. The AICTC upholds a strict Code of Ethics to ensure the highest standards of integrity and excellence among its members.

penalty applies when the Required Minimum Distribution (RMD)[2] is not taken.

## 2. Loss of control of your money.

You cannot access your money without paying a penalty and paying income tax on the amount you withdraw. Sometimes, someone else is in control of the performance of the investments you choose inside the retirement plan. You get no additional tax benefit if or when there are losses inside retirement plans. Since retirement plan funds are taxed when you take them out, you won't receive any of the traditional tax treatment and benefits typically featured with investments. Given that the government controls the laws regulating retirement accounts, they could change the laws at any time further restricting your access to your money or even forcing you to pay tax on those monies sooner than expected.

## 3. Paying higher taxes.

Since retirement accounts are tax-deferred, your tax rate is determined at the time you withdraw your money. Potentially, this means that at the time of withdrawal, you could be in a higher tax bracket than you were at the time you put money into your account. This can happen as a result of at least two things. First, you realize you need more money than you estimated for your retirement and must take a job when you retire. This keeps your income at a higher level and therefore your tax rate is higher as well. Second, income tax rates could increase for your retirement level of income due to tax law changes.

## 4. Inherited Retirement Accounts.

Heirs and beneficiaries many times pre-spend their inherited retirement account before finding out it is taxable. They fail to take the money out in a way that minimizes the amount of tax due. They don't

---

2 RMDs Required Minimum Distributions are generally the annual minimum amount of money you must take out of your (including inherited accounts) IRAs and other qualified employer plans like the 401K to avoid the IRS assessing and you paying a 50% penalty on the amount not taken out when required. Generally this starts the year the individual reaches age 70½. For 401Ks, there are specific instructions on how the RMD is calculated in IRS Publication 575.

realize they have options. Many just take a lump sum and pay the maximum amount of tax. Again they don't realize adding this income to their existing income pushes them into paying a higher percentage in taxes.

**Now that some of the basic retirement plan pitfalls have been explained in detail, here are three real life situations to illustrate how your 401K might end up plotting against you.**

Have you heard of any of the following happening to you or someone you know?

## Business Capital Needed

One of my clients, a married couple, faithfully made contributions to their retirement plan for a few years. At the time of making these contributions they were paying approximately 15% federal tax on income not put into the plan; so they were giving up the ability to pay tax on that money at a 15% rate. Last year the wife, who had been developing a new business, needed more money to expand the business. In the same year the husband was offered a position at a new company making more money. The couple assumed they had no other real options to get more money and they cashed in their account prematurely (before age 59½). They ended up paying 38% of their withdrawal in taxes and penalty. Of the $43,000 they took out of the plan, they received only $26,660 ($43,000 less $4,300 (10% early withdrawal penalty) less $12,040 (28% income tax)). Their income tax rate increased to 28% because their overall income increased due to the additional income from the retirement distribution.

Had they consulted with me and done careful planning, I would have advised them to just put their money into a savings account (exclusive of any interest earnings) rather than the retirement account. Doing so would have looked like this: total available $43,000 less income tax paid at 15% ($6,450) equals $36,550. The couple lost out on $9,890 they did not have to pay.

## Inherited 401K Surprise!

One of my clients inherited his dad's 401K when his dad passed unexpectedly. My client's first surprise was that he was going to have to pay tax when he took the money out of the 401K he had inherited. He thought it was a tax-free inheritance. Unfortunately, retirement plans do not pass tax free to the heirs or beneficiaries. Against my advice he took all the money out during a two year period instead of doing a rollover into an Inherited IRA[3] and taking the monies out over his life expectancy or some other more tax advantaged way. His second surprise was when he took the money out; it increased his tax rate to the highest percentage tax bracket because the amount he took out of the 401K raised his overall income.

Depending on the specific retirement plan and whether you are the spouse or a non-spouse beneficiary you have a range of options to take the money out of the plan. Some of the possible options are continuing a pre-established series of payments out of the plan setup by the decedent prior to his death, receiving payments over your life expectancy, doing a rollover into an Inherited IRA or even taking out the entire balance and paying your current income tax rates on the amount of the distribution.

## Withdrawing Retirement Money Too Late

One of my colleagues had a client who started with him a few years after the client's husband had passed away. Part of what her husband had left her was his retirement account, which allowed her to take the proceeds over her own life expectancy. After her husband's passing, she reached age 70½. What this woman didn't realize is the law required her to withdraw "Required Minimum Distributions" (RMD). As a result she was assessed a 50% penalty for failure to take the RMD. Fortunately, due to some unique medical situations during this period and a plan to prevent this from happening again in the future, a waiver of the 50% penalty was applied for and granted. By working with a qualified professional, the woman saved the 50% penalties she otherwise owed.

---

3 A special IRA separate from any other IRA used to rollover the monies a non-spouse inherits from a 401K of a decedent.

The above three stories illustrate some of the problems that can and have occurred when the rules are either not followed correctly and/or not known to the participants. This is not to say retirement accounts are bad, just that they may not be the best option based on your situation and goals.

So how do you decide if participating in a retirement plan is right for you? I created a list below of questions you should ask yourself.

# Is a Retirement Plan right for me?

Answer these questions:

1. Will I be in a lower percentage tax bracket when I take the money out of the plan than when I put it in?
    a. If you have planned your finances such that you are virtually debt free when you retire and know that you can live on the amount of income that keeps your retirement tax rate less than or equal to what it was when you put your money into your plan, then a retirement plan could be a good option for you.
    b. When you retire if you expect your income to be at a level where your tax rate is higher than when you put the money into the plan, a retirement plan is probably not a good option.
2. Is my employer matching my contribution in some way?
    a. If not, 401K is probably not a good option.
    b. If so, then depending on the percentage of match it could be a great option if your answers to the rest of these questions also indicate it is.
3. Will I need access to the money in my retirement plan before age 59½?
    a. If yes, probably not a good option.
    b. If no, then it may be a good option.
4. Am I planning on taking any loans from my retirement plan or cashing it out before age 59½?
    a. If yes, probably not a good option.

   b.  If no, then it may be a good option.

5.  Do I have other places I could invest the money where I could earn more than what I am earning in the plan, including my current tax rate while still showing a profit?

   a.  If yes, then a retirement plan is probably not a good option.

   b.  If no, then it may be a good option.

As you have probably determined by now there may not be an absolute clear answer for your specific situation. However, after answering the above five questions, you should have more confidence in knowing whether a retirement plan would work for you given your circumstances, beliefs and feelings. The best way to find out if a retirement plan is right for you is to meet with a Certified Tax Coach who can address your specific situation and give you their recommendations.

## Some Commonly Asked Questions

- **How can you withdraw your money before age 59½ without paying a penalty?**

   1.  If you have an **immediate and heavy financial need**[4] and it is **necessary to satisfy that financial need**[5]. When these re-

---

4   A distribution is deemed to be on account of an immediate and heavy financial need of the employee if the distribution is for:
   - Expenses for medical care previously incurred by the employee, the employee's spouse, or any dependents of the employee or necessary for these persons to obtain medical care;
   - Costs directly related to the purchase of a principal residence for the employee (excluding mortgage payments);
   - Payment of tuition, related educational fees, and room and board expenses, for the next 12 months of postsecondary education for the employee, or the employee's spouse, children, or dependents;
   - Payments necessary to prevent the eviction of the employee from the employee's principal residence or foreclosure on the mortgage on that residence;
   - Funeral expenses; or
   - Certain expenses relating to the repair of damage to the employee's principal residence.

5   A distribution may not be treated as **necessary to satisfy an immediate and heavy financial need** of an employee to the extent the amount of the distribution

quirements are met, a 401(k) plan may allow employees to receive a hardship distribution.

2. You are separated from the service of the 401K plan employer and you have set up a payment schedule to withdraw money in substantially equal amounts over the course of your life expectancy. (Once you begin taking this kind of distribution you are required to continue for five years or until you reach age 59½, whichever is longer.)

You will still pay the income tax on the amounts taken out from either of the two above methods. Remember by taking these kinds of distributions, this added income may increase the percentage of tax you'll pay on these distributions too.

- **What if I am already in a retirement plan and have decided I do not want to continue to participate?**

   You can elect to stop making contributions at any time (except for certain defined benefit plans). You can then take that same money and:

1. At the very least put the money in an interest bearing savings account.

2. Put it in a Roth IRA, if you meet the Roth IRA requirements.

3. If a Roth IRA won't work for you, you could purchase a certain type of dividend paying life insurance contract as discussed in the book *Becoming Your Own Banker: Unlock the Infinite Banking Concept* by R. Nelson Nash. Basically, it can act like an unlimited Roth IRA, without the income or contribution limitations of a standard Roth IRA.

4. If you have a successful business you are passionate about and feel confident about what you're doing, you could invest in that business.

---

is in excess of the amount required to relieve the financial need or to the extent the need may be satisfied from other resources that are reasonably available to the employee.

The main idea here is to do things with your money so you have more control over it, and it would be more profitable than putting it into a retirement plan (if you see a retirement plan may not be the best kind of retirement product for you).

- **What options do I have for the money I already have in 401K(s)?**

  Assuming you no longer work for the company(s) that have the 401K(s) and the plan(s) allow it, some of the options are:

  1. Roll them over, tax free, into an IRA, if you follow the rules.
  2. Leave them in the plan until age 59½ or retirement.
  3. Take out the money and pay the income tax and 10% penalty.
  4. Take the money out as part of a series of substantially equal periodic payments (made at least annually) for your life (or life expectancy) or the joint lives (or joint life expectancies) of you and your designated beneficiary.

- **What can I do instead of a retirement plan?**

  1. A Roth IRA. You pay tax at your current tax rate and if you follow the rules you pay no tax on the earnings. (See Chapter Eight on Roth IRAs).
  2. Certain dividend-paying life insurance contracts, when used properly can act like an unlimited Roth IRA and with much more freedom to access your monies.
  3. Invest to expand a current successful business you have control of.
  4. Check out fixed annuities.

# Glossary of Words, Terms, and Phrases

**401K** – A retirement plan made available by a company to its employees. Employees and employer can put money into the plan before paying income taxes on the money. Any growth or earnings in the account grow income tax deferred. Employers usually provide investment options the employees can select from to have their money invested in. Taxes are paid when monies are taken out of the plan, unless it meets the requirements of being treated as a loan.

**Beneficiary** – A person or entity named in a will or a financial contract as the inheritor of property (in this case the 401K) when the property owner dies.

**Decedent** – A person who has died.

**Distribution** – A payment of monies from a tax deferred account, like a 401K, to the individual account owner.

**Life expectancy** – The expected (in the statistical sense) number of years of life remaining at a given age.

**Rollover** – A method used to move money from one tax-deferred retirement account to another without having to pay tax on the monies so transferred.

**Tax-deferred** – Tax-deferred investments in particular refer to retirement accounts which allow deferral of income taxes on contributions into the plan and growth. Taxes are not paid until money is taken out of the plan.

# Craig E. Waldron, EA, CTC

President & Owner

Tax & Accounting Solutions Corporation

dba Padgett Business Services Salt Lake
   9500 South 500 West, Suite 206
   Sandy, UT 84070

Craig Waldron serves as a recognized tax and small business expert for doctors, dentists, business owners, and executives from California to Maine. As a successful business owner he has served as president of Padgett Business Services – Salt Lake City, Utah since 1997. He first started helping people stop wasting unnecessary taxes during his first tax season in 1974. He meets with his clients and business owners to identify where clients are losing $1000s unnecessarily to inefficient tax planning strategies and implementation. He then resolves these issues through proactive tax planning and correct implementation. He loves to create solutions to get doctors, businesses, and individuals from where they are to where they want to be.

Prior to starting his Padgett Business Services tax and accounting firm, Craig worked as the Vice President of Technology and Finance for the Clements Group national consulting group, whose purpose was to train the local development staffs of each institution to raise funds for infrastructure improvement and new construction on Junior College campuses on a nationwide level. As a result, these colleges raised multi-millions of dollars for these purposes.

He is a graduate of Weber State University with a B.S. degree in Accounting, an Enrolled Agent, Certified QuickBooks ProAdvisor, Author, and a Certified Tax Coach.

Craig has a highly qualified team of CPAs, accountants and tax attorneys to use as resources to resolve even the toughest issues of small businesses, including their tax and accounting needs. His philosophy is to do what is best for the client always. Craig is also a tenacious achiever with a broad range of experience in the professional services industry as well as having excellent interpersonal, negotiation and communication skills.

To find out how you can pay less tax call Craig at 801-565-9878 or e-mail him at craig@taxpainrelief.com. To get additional free information go to www.taxpainrelief.com Click on the Tax Strategies tab or get a free monthly newsletter about the latest in issues affecting small businesses at the above website by clicking on the left hand column of the page NEWS> Monthly Newsletter.

# CHAPTER EIGHT

# The Roth IRA: The Real Secret to Tax Free Living!

### By Robert A. Gambardella, CPA CTC

"Free" is one of those catchy words that is thrown around a bit too often, especially in advertising. It's used so much that it starts to lose its luster after a while. After all, nothing in life is truly "free," is it? Even the title of this book likely caught your attention because: Who wouldn't want to live life tax-free? But is it really possible? There are tons of great ideas in this book to get your tax bill significantly reduced (and I hope you use every one of them!), but there are only a select handful that you can actually use to pay zero tax at all.

I'd like to introduce you to a spectacular investment vehicle called the Roth IRA. What? You've already heard of those? Maybe you already have one, or stopped contributing to one at some point because your income level exceeded the allowable contribution thresholds. Or maybe you thought about contributing to one at some point. After all, it's the *thought* that counts, right? Well let me tell you, that old dog of a Roth IRA lying in the corner is capable of all kinds of tricks. Let's explore!

# Roth IRA: Background and Basics

Q: What Exactly is a Roth IRA?

A: A Roth IRA is a retirement account that gives you a tax break on the amounts withdrawn, rather than the amounts you contribute. This big difference compared to other types of retirement plans opens the door to some truly unique tax planning opportunities.

Q: How Much Can I Contribute?
A: Up to $5,000 of <u>earned</u> income can be contributed on an after tax basis annually. The limit is $6,000 if you are at least age 60.

Q: What is The Tax Treatment of My Contributions, Earnings, and Withdrawals?

- Your original contributions aren't tax deductible, so they are made with after-tax dollars. After that, they are generally tax-free for life and can be accessed any time penalty-free!
- At any time, you can convert IRA funds into Roth IRA funds. The catch? You pay tax on the amount you convert based on your tax rate for the year in which you make the conversion.
- Earnings on your Roth savings are tax free after age 59 ½, and some useful exceptions allow you to access those earnings prior to age 59 ½.

Q: In Addition to Withdrawing My Original Contributions, How Can I Make Withdrawals Penalty-Free Before Age 59 ½?

- To buy or build a first home for self or family member, up to $10,000. The definition here is VERY forgiving. "First Home" is defined as a primary residence to someone who has not owned a home for at least 2 years.
- To pay for eligible medical expenses that were not reimbursed
- To pay for medical insurance premiums after a job loss
- To pay for higher education expenses
- Any withdrawals made after you become permanently disabled
- To pay taxes related to an IRS levy

- To take a short-term loan, as long as you roll the full amount over within 60 days (only allowed once per year)

**Important:** All of the above are subject to a five-year holding period.

Now that we've covered the basics, let's see what tax planning strategies are available to Roth IRA investors of all ages.

# Silly Rabbit: Roth IRA's Are For Kids!

Open Roth IRA's for your kids. Right now. (OK, maybe read the chapter first so you know why, but then go out and do it.) Getting started early is the name of the game in investing, we all know that. If you have the opportunity to start a savings fund for your children, strongly consider doing so inside of a Roth IRA. The secret to doing this is the child must have EARNED income. You can contribute up to $5,000 each year, or 100% of the amount of your child's earned income, whichever is lower. So if parents are having a tough time keeping their own jobs these days, exactly how will little Johnny go out and get one? Well, it certainly helps if his parents (you) also happen to be a business owner, or even a rental property owner. If you can find a role for your children to play in your business, by all means hire them and pay them a fair wage for their work! That gives you the qualifying earned income required to take advantage of the Roth IRA. Kids don't want to work? Consider other strategies to create earned income for them, such as a gift-leaseback arrangement (see Chapter Nine).

Why would a child want their savings locked up until age 59 ½? Well, a Roth IRA is more flexible than you think. Your contributions were made after-tax, so you can withdraw them at any time with no tax or penalties. Withdrawals can also be made penalty free for college expense or a first home for example. So getting a large sum of money into a Roth IRA at an early age allows for A LOT of tax flexibility later on in life. If you can build a substantial amount of earnings in the account over those first 18 years, they can essentially withdraw the original contributions during their college years or to help buy a home, and the rest of the account earnings or appreciation, let's call it the remaining "house money," can grow tax free until their retirement!

Let's illustrate: By contributing $5,000 per year to a Roth IRA for the first 18 years of your child's life, you would accumulate $90K of contributions. If the account grew at a rate of 8% per year, the total account balance would be $200K at age 18. They could withdraw $90K for college and $10K towards a first home tax and penalty-free. The remaining $100K can continue to grow tax free. At age 65, even if ZERO additional contributions to the account were made, the account would grow to nearly $4M[1] . If they continued to qualify for $5,000 per year contributions up to age 65, that account balance would grow to $6.5M! And every dollar could be withdrawn during retirement TAX FREE! (under current tax law of course).

Are you starting to see the power of the Roth IRA?

# Your Working Years: Preparing For a Tax-Free Retirement

So here you are reading this and thinking to yourself, "man, I wish my parents had opened a Roth IRA for me as a kid. But they never received such proactive tax planning advice. So I sit here today mid-career wondering what I can still do to take advantage of a Roth IRA."

Well, there are all sorts of ways to create tax-free retirement income for yourself during your working years. The name of the game is all about tax brackets: your current tax bracket, and your expected tax bracket during retirement. If your tax rate today is higher than you believe it will be in retirement, then you are likely better off putting your savings in a traditional IRA or a 401K plan. But if you expect your tax rate to be higher during retirement than it is today, make those contributions to a Roth IRA first. Of course, your tax rate can change from year to year depending on your business, so this is an analysis you need to do annually. I see too many people blindly maxing out their annual 401K contributions, which potentially becomes a ticking time bomb for them, since they will eventually pay tax on those funds upon withdrawing them. In today's economic climate, who knows what the tax rates will even be in 10, 20, or 30 years? Honestly, if I have a chance

---

1   Assumed 8% rate of return.

to pay 15% tax on my annual $5,000 Roth IRA contribution, I gladly will, knowing that if I put those same funds in a 401K plan, I may end up paying 25% or more on the same money (and the related earnings) during retirement.

Here are the tax planning opportunities you need to be on the lookout for when looking for ways to contribute to a Roth IRA:

- **Convert in "Down" Years:** If your business start-up loses money in year 1, or you will show a loss or small gain due to major equipment investment, non-recurring expenses, or bonus depreciation, then you have a golden opportunity to convert as much IRA money as possible into a Roth IRA account. Imagine offsetting a $50,000 business loss with a $50,000 IRA conversion, not paying tax on the conversion, and not paying tax on that balance or its earnings when you withdraw it during retirement? Make the most of your business losses! Similarly, a wage earner has this same unique opportunity in years they find themselves between jobs or lose their jobs due to company down-sizing. When life deals you those lemons, consider the Roth IRA conversion opportunity to turn those losses into lemonade!

- **Convert Over Time:** Are you finding enough great tax –saving ideas in this book that you can get yourself down into a lower tax bracket every year? Any opportunity you have to pay only 10% or 15%, or even 20% tax, it might be a perfectly good idea to do so! Picking your own tax rate can be as much fun as using Priceline.com. I would perform an analysis once per year to see how much you can convert up to the top of the tax bracket of your choice, and slowly over time, convert those IRA dollars over to your Roth IRA account. A brilliant way to escape future tax increases!

- **The Do-Over:** When you make Roth IRA conversions, remember, you are choosing to pay some tax today on the rollover amount, to avoid paying more tax on the same amount later. You can hedge this bet a little, by opening multiple Roth IRA accounts, each with its own distinct investment objective. You can then allocate your rollover funds into these multiple accounts.

Why would you do that? Well, you are allowed to unwind any Roth IRA rollover by October 15 of the following year. So if the market drops, or in this case, a particular industry or two, you can unwind only the portions of your rollover that lost money that year, claim the capital loss as a tax deduction, and try the rollover again another time!

- **Hold Property Inside Your Roth:** Did you know you can own a rental property inside your Self-Directed Roth IRA? That's right, it's not only stocks, bonds, and mutual funds we're talking about here. You can invest in just about anything with your Roth. It is actually a complex process to set something like that up, but is well worth the effort. Imagine buying a property in the current market, and earning rental income and capital appreciation tax-free over a number of years, and leaving that property to your children tax-free. That's an incredible opportunity worth considering!

# Roth IRA's and The Tax-Free Retirement

There's no worse feeling than finding out after a hard-working career that your social security benefits can become taxable if the amount you withdraw from an IRA or 401K account to meet your desired lifestyle exceeds certain thresholds. Well, that can be avoided if you accumulate as much of your retirement savings as possible within a Roth IRA. See, the tax on those amounts was "prepaid" when you made the contribution. You may even have been fortunate enough to convert in years where you had a 0% tax bracket and you never paid tax on those funds at all! Roth IRA withdrawals are not taxable income after you reach age 59 1/2, so those amounts won't factor in to the taxability calculation of your social security benefits.

I've seen people who have retired and withdrawn significant amounts from their 401K to purchase a retirement home, only to be surprised with a massive tax bill (which required them to make even further taxable withdrawals just to pay the tax!). Don't get caught in that position, your retirement savings can be depleted rather quickly.

And the last thing you want is to return to work, I've seen that happen too.

By proactively saving for your retirement in the most tax-efficient way, the benefits you reap from funding your retirement through a Roth IRA can be substantial. It is actually possible to live tax-free throughout your retirement if you work this strategy perfectly over the course of your working years. A summary of the advantages is below:

- Interest, dividends, and capital gains earned in the Roth IRA are tax-free

- Withdrawals from your Roth IRA beyond age 59 ½ are tax-free

- You can maximize your social security benefits by drawing from your Roth IRA up to age 65 and delaying social security benefits until you can collect the maximum benefit

- You can escape taxability of your social security benefits by drawing the remainder of your annual income from a non-taxable source

- You can avoid taxable income spikes, in tax years where you need to withdraw significant amounts to cover medical expenses or other major expenses, for example

- Your heirs and beneficiaries pay no income tax on their inherited share of your Roth IRA savings. This is a big one. When you leave behind $1 Million in a Roth IRA, your heirs keep $1 Million. If they inherit the same $1M in a traditional IRA or a 401K account, they may be left with $400,000 to $600,000 after taxes. That's a big difference!

Entire books can be written on the tax advantages and planning strategies related to Roth IRA's, so I hope this brief chapter was enough to at least whet your appetite. Making the best use of your Roth IRA account can significantly reduce the amount of tax you pay over your lifetime, and in some cases you can truly live tax-free! So make sure you are considering Roth IRA contributions each tax year, and determine when it is most appropriate to make conversions from other account types as well. Maybe there aren't really TWO things certain in life after all!

# Robert Gambardella, CPA CTC

Robert Gambardella is a CPA and Certified Tax Coach, and has been the Principal of Concierge Tax Services, LLC since 2005, based in Shelton, CT. As "CT's Most Proactive CPA," Robert's practice focuses on tax planning first, and provides full-service tax preparation and accounting only after upfront and immediate value has been delivered in the form of a Proactive Tax Plan. A true financial "triple threat," Robert has held advanced roles in the 3 key areas of Controllership, Finance, and Tax at companies such as Perkinelmer Inc., GE Capital Commercial Finance, and PricewaterhouseCoopers LLP.

Robert graduated from Quinnipiac University with a Bachelor's Degree in Accounting, and is a member of the AICPA, AICTC, and CTSCPA. In delivering on his company motto, "Thrill The Client," he is relentless in identifying legal tax-saving strategies, and is meticulous in delivering his ideas and recommendations in a simple, easy-to-understand format. He is an active member of his local community, and recently ran in his first marathon!

For more information about Robert Gambardella's services, and to setup an appointment, visit his website at www.ConciergeTax.com, or give him a call directly at 203-767-7197.

# CHAPTER NINE

# How to Deduct Your Kids' Soccer Cleats (Hint: Give Them a Seat at the Board Room Table!)

By Craig S. Cody, CPA CTC

So what's the best way to deduct your kid's soccer cleats?? How about giving them a seat on your board of directors! Maybe you don't want your 7-year-old child making decisions that can affect the life of your business. How about hiring your child? (Make them an employee!)

Did you know that your child can earn up to $5,800 before they pay taxes on their income? Are you paying more than that? This income shifting technique allows you to enjoy a tax deduction for the wages you pay your kids (saving your tax bill while adding no additional tax for them!) Their next $8,500 in income is only taxed at a rate of 10%. Ask yourself again, are you paying more than 10%? Even better, earned income is not subject to the kiddie tax.

You might be wondering how you can accomplish this, while not running afoul of the IRS. First, you must really employ your child! But including Jr. in your workload may be easier than you think. Just follow these simple steps:

1. **Create an agreement between your business and your child.** The agreement should spell out what job functions the child should perform. The tax court has approved wages for children as young as 7 years old. The work they perform should be directly related to your business and the wage they earn should be reasonable for their age and the work that is performed. I have seen young employees that handle licking envelopes, filing, data input and answering the phones on the weekends. It is important that the agreement be clear and concise when it spells out the child's job description.

2. **Keep good records**: You must be able to substantiate your deduction and you should do this by having your child keep a timesheet showing the dates, times, and services performed. It is always a good idea to review the timesheet at the end of every pay period with the employee and have them sign off on the total hours worked. As the owner and employer, you must be willing to make sure the time worked is well documented. I have had some clients that include the task of having the timesheet reviewed by the business owner in the employee's job description.

3. **Pay your child**: Always pay your child by check or direct deposit and make sure the salary goes into an account in the child's name. This account can be a custodial account[1], a section 529 savings plan or a Roth IRA.

I had a client come into my office looking for a tax plan so that he could reduce the amount of taxes he was paying every year. In going over this particular client's situation I discovered that the business owner already had his little 8-year-old son, who I will refer to as Johnny, working for him, but little Johnny wasn't being paid. The business owner would take his 8-year-old son into his office every Saturday and Johnny would place mailing labels on the company's weekly mailers.

---

1 Assets in custodial accounts cannot be used for your obligations of parental support, but can be used for items like private school tuition, summer camps and similar items.

As part of his tax plan, I recommended my client hire little Johnny and he paid his son $8 per hour for 4 hours every week. At the end of the year we saw that Johnny was paid over $1,500 and my client who was paying taxes at a federal and state combined rate of about 33%, saved over $500 in taxes from this one strategy alone.

If that savings doesn't appeal to you let me tell you about my client with twins in private high school with annual tuition of approximately $8,000 per year. Up until the point that the business owner came to me he was paying $16,000 in high school tuition every year without receiving any tax deductions for this expense. His daughters had been working in his office for the last 3 summers full time and receiving an allowance from dad in return.

After we completed the tax plan for this business owner, he decided to put his 2 girls on the company payroll. The girls each came into their Dad's office 1 day a week after school for 2 hours, they worked another 2 hours remotely, saving the company e-fax's to the client files (yes, dad had his office on "the cloud") and came in for another 4 hours every other Saturday. This plus the time they spent working in dad's office during the summer totaled 652 hours a year and at $12 per hour totaled $7,824 in wages for each of the girls each year. The girls were paid every 2 weeks direct deposit into their custodial accounts and the private high school drafted the child's account once per month for $800, one-tenth of the annual tuition. Dad was also effectively paying a combined federal and state tax rate of 33% so dad reduced his tax bill by $5,280. This new found tax savings effectively reduced the cost of the private school tuition by approximately 30%.

You may be saying, I don't have a traditional business with an office so how else may I hire my kids?? I prepared a tax plan for a client who was a real estate investor. He owned 2 residential rental properties within walking distance of his home and a third property down the shore near his vacation home. He hired his son (Big Johnny) his junior year in high school to take over some of the property management functions. Big Johnny was responsible for depositing the monthly rent checks into the individual LLC's bank accounts every month. His other responsibilities included driving by twice a week and taking a picture of the outside of the property with his iPhone and emailing the photo to dad. This allowed dad to keep a keen eye on the curb appeal of his investment. During the summer, Big Johnny would be responsible for mowing the lawn and doing the weekly gardening as well as walking through the shore property at the end of the weekly rental after the cleaning service had finished their cleaning. Big Johnny would fill out an online report and email it to dad along with pictures of any suspected damage. Dad paid Big Johnny the same fee he would have paid a property manager and a landscaper. Dad saved a bunch of taxes and Big Johnny gained responsibility and learned some valuable life skills while being able to contribute money to his section 529 College Savings Plan at the same time.

You may say that sounds good but what about payroll taxes? Check out this attractive tax break on payroll taxes: businesses organized as sole proprietorships don't owe social security or medicare taxes on their minor children's wages until they reach the age of 18 and you don't owe unemployment taxes in most states until your child reaches 21. If your business is organized as a partnership and you and your spouse own 100% of the partnership interests the same rules apply.

Don't overlook the expenses of your grown children in your tax plan! These days more and more children in their 20's and 30's are returning to "the nest" due to economic difficulties and high unemployment rates. If you are providing financial support, this expense can help lower your taxes by including your children in your business. Begin by looking at your child's tax rate. Is their tax bracket lower than your tax bracket? If it is, you may want to shift income down to their bracket. This is easy to accomplish following my advice above, but you might also consider making your children a shareholder of your business.

Partnerships, LLCs, and S corporations are known as "pass-through" entities. That is, the profits and losses of the business "pass-through" to its owners who pay tax based on their own individual rates. Taking advantage of this structure you can shift income to your children by including them as shareholders or partners in your business.

While this strategy might appear easy, beware of a few considerations. First, check with your state regulations, your child may need to be older than age 18 in order to enter into any legal agreements such as shareholder or partnership agreements. Also of note for minor children are the kiddie tax rules. The kiddie tax rules require children who receive more than $1,700 per year in unearned income to pay tax at their parent's tax rates. Given this obstacle, if you attempt to shift income by making your 17-year-old dependent child a shareholder of your S corporation, you may end up paying the same amount of tax on your own tax return! Despite these disadvantages, this strategy of making your adult children a part of the ownership of your business can create thousands in tax savings each year. This strategy may also help in your plan to minimize estate tax. Be sure to work with a strong proactive tax planner to assist you in building these plans around your specific needs.

Visit my website at www.TaxCoachNY.com and you will find a running total of the taxes I have saved clients, additionally, opt in for my weekly emails and you will receive more examples of tax saving strategies for your business.

# Craig S. Cody, CPA CTC

I was born and raised on Long Island, NY. In between doing what average suburban kids do, I spent much of my childhood at the heels of my father who retired from the NYC Police Department after 33 years, and who currently resides in South Florida with my mother. My mother, whose roots are in Brooklyn where she met my father, is a retired legal assistant.

My interest in the financial world led me to major in Economics in college. My interest in financial independence at age 21 (and in following in Dad's footsteps), led me to a 17-year career with the New York City Police Department.

I retired as a Lieutenant from the NYC Police Department in September 2000. I became a licensed CPA in September 2002 after working for two years for an international CPA firm. In September 2003, I added public accounting services to my growing financial services practice, which has now been in existence for 10 years.

My CPA practice has evolved over time and is now split between proactive tax planning, small business accounting, and tax preparation. I have developed a niche market in proactive tax planning strategies. I find the prospect of teaching my clients ways to reduce their tax burden rewarding, and although hectic at times, it is what I enjoy the most. No two days are alike.

I am proud to say I have three healthy, kind, and active children, ages 21, 19, and 17, and have been married for 22 years.

# CHAPTER TEN

# Beat Rising Medical Costs: Beyond Healthcare Savings Accounts (HSAs)

### By Barbara Richardson, CPA CTC

M edical costs are increasing faster than income. According to a report published by the Kaiser Family Foundation and the Health Research & Educational Trust, premiums have increased 131 percent since 1999 and 2011 has seen the cost of employer-provided plans increase by 9% - even as doctor visits decline. Although Congress recently passed the Patient Protection and Affordable Care Act (aka ObamaCare), medical costs are expected to continue rising. The continued increases in costs have no doubt encouraged many people to look for ways to save on these costs, such as switching to qualified High Deductible Plans. Others look to tax benefits to finance the costs by taking advantage of medical tax breaks such as Healthcare Savings Accounts, or HSAs.

While most taxpayers have a basic understanding that medical expenses are deductible as an itemized deduction on schedule A of their individual tax return, what they do NOT realize is that these expenses are only deductible to the extent that they exceed over 7.5% of their adjusted gross income! For example, let's say that you earn $100,000 per year and spend $8,000 in out of pocket medical expenses. Under the current rules for itemizing your deductions, just $500 of your medical expenses are deductible! ($8,000 less 7.5% of income).Most people just don't have that many in deductions, and even for those that do, most of the expense is lost due to the rule.

One way around this rule is to look for alternative tax breaks for medical costs. An HSA by definition is a tax-advantaged medical savings account available to those who are enrolled in a qualified high deductible health insurance plan (HDHP), and provides a means for deducting out of pocket medical costs. Taxpayers can deposit money into their Health Savings Account. They receive a tax deduction for the amounts contributed and distributions are tax free as long as they are used for qualified medical expenses. In other words, you create your own tax deductible savings account and reimburse yourself tax free for your medical expenses. These HSAs provide other attractive features such as no use-it-or-lose-it provision, and funds can accumulate and roll over year to year. The current annual maximum amount that can be contributed to an HSA as a tax deduction is $3,100 for an individual and $6,250 for a family as of 2012. While an HSA is good and provides some tax deductions for medical expenses as I've described above, a Section 105 or MERP is great if you qualify because it can provide a much larger tax deduction for business owners.

A Medical Expense Reimbursement Plan, or MERP, is an excellent way to deduct medical expenses. MERPs continue to be a popular strategy for proactive tax planning. If you are a business owner and your current tax advisor has not recommended this strategy to you, and it is possible that you qualify for it, run! It is almost always a great opportunity for closely held businesses, service oriented businesses such as insurance or real estate agents, as well as businesses with primarily part-time employees. A MERP can also work for other entities as well including larger companies or companies with many employees with proper planning. The reason MERPs are such a powerful tax planning strategy is because they allow you to deduct 100% of your qualifying medical costs as a business expense for employees. Not only does this deduction save income tax dollars, it can also help reduce some of the other specialty taxes discussed in this book such as self-employment tax, accumulated earnings tax, and personal service tax. One of the major benefits of implementing a MERP is that you are able to deduct medical expenses for the employee, their spouse and dependents. While most taxpayers deduct their medical expenses and lose 7.5% of their total income as a tax break, medical expenses through a MERP are not subject to the 7.5% floor for itemized deductions.

Unlike an HSA, MERPs can be used to supplement a spouse's medical coverage and MERPs do not have mandatory contributions because funds are only paid if the employee submits a qualified reimbursable expense. If you've ever found it difficult to estimate your annual medical expenses, relax! With the MERP, there is no "use it or lose it" rule. You deduct only what you incur, no estimating required!

Expenses eligible for reimbursement under a MERP include:

- Major medical, LTC, Medicare and Medigap insurance premiums
- Copays, deductibles and prescriptions
- Dental, vision and chiropractic
- Braces, LASIK, fertility and special schools
- Nonprescription medication (with a prescription)

Nonprescription medication is one of my favorites. This provision has allowed for the cost of a hot tub to be reimbursed because a client's chiropractor prescribed it to treat a leg injury, and has also provided a tax deduction for an 8-year-old's tae kwon do lessons because his pediatrician prescribed it as part of a treatment plan for ADHD. That is the charm of a MERP — it takes dollars that were going to be spent anyway and transforms them into tax free dollars, saving you both income and self-employment taxes.

## How to Qualify

Because a MERP is an employee benefit plan, it has to be offered to a bona fide employee. The following table illustrates how each business entity qualifies for the plan:

| Business Entity | How to Qualify |
|---|---|
| Proprietorship | Hire Spouse |
| Partnership | Hire Spouse (if limited partner or <5% owner) |
| S-Corporation | >2% shareholder ineligible |
| C-Corporation | Hire Self |

## Qualifying as a proprietorship

As a proprietor, or sole business owner, by definition you are not an employee of the company so you would not qualify to implement a MERP. However, if you have a spouse or dependent, who could be a bona fide employee of your company, you can offer a MERP to them as an employee. Recall that one of the benefits of a MERP is the ability for a covered employee to extend those benefits to their spouse or dependent. As an example, John is married to Tammy and he owns a plumbing company as a sole proprietor with no employees. If he hires Tammy to do the bookkeeping and administrative work, she becomes an employee and John's plumbing company now qualifies to implement a MERP, which could be used to reimburse Tammy for both of their medical expenses.

## Qualifying as a partnership

As long as the spouse is a limited partner or owns less than 5% of the company, the same option applies as discussed for the proprietorship.

## Qualifying as an S-Corporation

Any shareholder who owns more than 2% of the company is ineligible. However, if the company has multiple streams of income, such as a doctor who sees patients and does speaking engagements, or alternatively the company can segregate functions such as marketing or administration, then an opportunity for a MERP may still exist. The business owner might consider forming a different type of business entity to manage the separate income stream. Essentially, you want to select an entity for the new business which gives more favorable tax treatment than the S corporation.

## Qualifying as a C-Corporation

The easiest entity of all in which to implement the MERP is the C-Corporation because C corporations provide a tax deduction for fringe benefits for the shareholders. You can simply hire yourself and qualify as the bona fide employee.

## Tax Savings

It is much easier to see the effects of a MERP in a real-life situation. Remember, without a MERP, most taxpayers generally do not qualify to deduct 100% of their medical expenses.

John & Tammy have taxable income of $100,000 before any medical deductions. They paid $2,400 in medical premiums and $6,000 in medical costs such as copays, deductibles, prescriptions, etc. from their healthcare savings account. For the sake of this example, we are only considering the tax savings associated with paying medical costs with an HSA compared to paying them through a MERP, no other deduction or assumption is considered. We will assume an effective income tax rate of 20%.

If John implemented a medical expense reimbursement plan for his plumbing company, he would realize a tax savings greater than **80%** on dollars he was already spending! I stated earlier but it bears repeating, the charm of a MERP is that it takes money that was going to be spent anyway and transforms it into tax free money, saving the taxpayer both income and self-employment taxes. As discussed in Chapter One, this is the most powerful form of tax planning.

| Medical Expenses | HSA Tax Savings | MERP Tax Savings |
|---|---|---|
| Premiums – $2,400 | | |
| Income Tax | $480 | $480 |
| FICA | $0 | $367 |
| Medical Costs –$6,000 | | |
| Income Tax | $1,200 | $1,200 |
| FICA | $0 | $918 |
| **Total Tax Savings** | $1,680 | **$2,965** |

## The Fine Print

There are a few things to keep in mind when determining if a medical reimbursement plan will work for you.

1.  **Nondiscrimination** – the plan must cover all eligible employees, however, you can exclude employees who:
    a.  are under the age of 25
    b.  work less than 35 hours a week
    c.  are seasonal or work less than 9 months a year
    d.  have less than 3 years of service

2.  **Controlled Group Rules** – if multiple companies are primarily owned by the same owner(s), company A can't provide generous benefits to their employees and exclude the employees of company B. For example, if Company A has 50 employees and Company B has 5 employees, but share the same majority ownership, if Company B offers a MERP to their 5 employees, a MERP has to be offered to Company A's employees as well.

3.  **Affiliated Service Groups** – exists when one business receives 50% or greater of its gross income from another business, they are treated as 1 business as it relates to benefits such as a MERP.

Implementing a medical expense reimbursement plan is a great tax planning strategy that often yields significant tax savings. Considering the fact that health care costs are expected to continue rising, one way to control those costs is to maximize every tax deduction available to you. Be sure to consult with a tax advisor who specializes in proactive tax planning to assess if and how a MERP would fit in your tax plan, ensure that it is implemented properly and that all compliance rules are met. If you do, it can be a great way to beat the cost of health care!

# Barbara D. Richardson, CPA, CTC

950 Eagles Landing Parkway, Suite 201
Stockbridge, Georgia 30281
(770) 507-2150

www.springwellfinancial.com

Barbara D. Richardson is the founding Principal of SpringWell Financial Solutions. With over eleven years of experience in taxation and accounting services, she created SpringWell Financial Solutions to cater to the specific needs of individuals and small businesses. Although Barbara is a proficient analyzer of numbers, it is engaging and connecting with her clients that she enjoys most, and it shows in her personal attention to each client's specific needs. Barbara is at her best helping clients determine and achieve their business and personal financial goals.

Licensed in 2003 as a Certified Public Accountant in the state of Georgia, Barbara began her public accounting career with PricewaterhouseCoopers in 1999 as an Associate and participant in the firm's Business Advisory Service and Leadership Program. While at PwC, she worked with clients in the financial services, manufacturing, and technology industries. Ms. Richardson was also an Assistant Vice President in the Financial Reporting & Controls and Capital Markets divisions of a top ten national bank.

Committed to educating, equipping, and empowering others to attain financial freedom, Barbara teaches clients that a key element to building and maintaining wealth is by managing taxes. Knowing that taxes are generally the second largest expense for most families, Barbara and SpringWell Financial Solutions take great concern with providing clients with strategic individual and business tax planning that will allow for maximized tax savings and wealth preservation. Leveraging comprehensive knowledge of tax law, coupled with tax planning experience, Barbara ensures clients receive personalized planning that will yield the greatest benefit and allow for an efficient tax reporting process.

Barbara's career journey is the origin of her distinct ability to turn the complexities of multi-tiered tax and accounting theory into understandable concepts for her clients, thereby creating practical solutions for them to achieve. Well-respected for her knowledge and customer focus, clients continually look forward to working with Ms. Richardson.

Outside of the office, Barbara is an active and engaged member of Stockbridge, Georgia and the Metro Atlanta areas. She can often be found pursuing her civic passion of serving as a Board Member and volunteer with Chosen Heirs, a nonprofit organization that fosters leadership skills in adolescents and volunteering at Helping In His Name, a local food pantry. She regularly supports the initiatives of Hosea Feed the Hungry & Homeless, the Atlanta Union Mission, and the American Cancer Society. For recreation, Barbara enjoys traveling, enhancing her health & wellness knowledge, and preparing unique vegetarian and vegan recipes.

# CHAPTER ELEVEN

# Discover Your Inner Sleuth by Uncovering Hidden Business Deductions

BY MRS. DIONNE JOSEPH THOMAS,
MBA, PMP, EA, CTC

There are several tax planning opportunities available to business owners and independent contractors to reduce their tax bill.

Just like you, I personally know a lot of people who became unemployed in this recession. But in times of great turmoil, innovation thrives. Many people invested their savings into their own home-based businesses and are now thriving. They are excited and happy with a personal sense of pride and satisfaction from being self employed. But this feeling is quickly replaced with fear and sometimes horror when I explain how much money they would be losing from their newly found income in taxes!

I continually emphasize to my clients the need to get started right in order to avoid costly tax mistakes. Proactive Tax Planning allows business owners and independent contractors the ability to create tax plans filled with personalized strategies to legally reduce their tax bill.

Many of my clients utilize both the tax planning and maintenance services together, such as the Harris family. They enjoy prepaid tax consultations which allow them to update their tax strategies as life changes occur.

Previously, the Harris family tax plan was based upon an annual income of $170,000. But they achieved monumental success and their projected annual income is now $350,000. The bad news is now their tax rate is higher at 33%. (The actual client names and figures have been altered to protect their privacy.)

# Hidden Business Deductions

Business owners enjoy many more tax deductions as they can deduct expenses that would otherwise be classified as personal expenses for individuals.

For any expenditure to be deductible, though, it must be "ordinary and necessary" in your line of business. **Ordinary expenses** are those expenses generally accepted as part of doing business in your industry. **Necessary expenses** are generally accepted as expenses that facilitate the smooth operation and are required in your line of business. Therefore with Proactive Tax Planning just about anything can be a deduction, if it helps your business!

To truly maximize savings and take legitimate hidden business deductions, business owners must have the receipts, invoices and other records to back up their claims.

# Hidden Business Deductions: The Home Office Deduction

Both owners and renters may be able to deduct a portion of the costs of their home if it is used for business. To deduct the "business use of home" expense you must regularly and exclusively dedicate a portion of your home as either:

- The principal place of business and/or
- Exclusively as the place to interact with customers, patients, or clients in your regular business operations, or

- In direct association with your business(if you utilize a structure that is not attached to your home or residence).

To satisfy the exclusive-use rule, ensure that the portion of the room(s) used for business purposes are separately identifiable spaces. You cannot deduct expenses for the business use of your home if the designated area is used for both business and personal reasons.

The Harris family operates a marketing consulting home based business. They use their home office for substantial managerial and administrative activities (billing customers, scheduling appointments, etc), since they have no other fixed location to perform these activities. Their home office is treated as their principal place of business.

There are two types of expenses related to a home office:

1. **Direct Expenses** – Expenses related exclusively to the business are fully deductible. These can include things like, business insurance, general repairs, improvements, service or maintenance to facilitate business operations. *Example: Furnishing the home office.*

2. **Indirect Expenses** – The percentage of general home expenses attributed to the operations of the business, otherwise known as the "Business Use Percentage." *Example; the portion of the electricity bill attributed to the business.* BUP (Business Use Percentage) = Square footage of office/total finished square footage of home or apartment.  If your business is 20% of your home you can deduct 20% of your home bills!

Indirect expenses can include the following:

- Mortgage Interest
- Real Estate taxes
- Depreciation
- Rent
- Utilities (Gas, electric, water, and sewer)
- Insurance (Homeowner's)

The Harris family uses one of their five rooms for business. Since their rooms are more or less the same size, and they use a full room for business, they can use the rooms method. Therefore we allocated 20 percent of expenses (1/5), for their business. Otherwise we would allocate the expenses based on the BUP.

**Tax Savings Opportunity #1:**

The "rooms method" ( 1/5 rooms = 20%) yields a bigger deduction than the square-footage method (300 sq. ft./ 2500 sq. ft. 12%). By using the "rooms method," the Harris family are now able to deduct more of their business expenses from their income.

**Change from BUP to Rooms method increased the home deduction expenses to $35,000.**

**Tax Savings Opportunity #2:**

Auto deductions do not include driving for personal reasons, therefore commuting is considered a personal expense and is not deductible. The Harris family uses their home office as their primary place of business, therefore every trip the Harris family takes to meet a client is fully deductible. **All of their business travel miles are deductible to and from their office!**

# Hidden Business Deductions: Section 179 deduction

Normally business property even though it is purchased in one year, the cost must be depreciated over a period of time, often spanning multiple tax years. First-year expensing or Section 179 deduction is a special depreciation allowance for small businesses to fully deduct property in its first year of service.

Business property qualifies for Section 179 deduction by meeting the following requirements:

- The property must be tangible(off-the-shelf computer software included)
- The property must be acquired for business use
- The property must be acquired by purchase (the property cannot be gifted)

Section 179 deductions provide small business owners with an opportunity to maximize the deduction for their business assets. This strategy is not ideal for all circumstances. Discuss this strategy thoroughly with your tax consultant before proceeding.

Limitations of Section 179 deductions:

- Your Section 179 deductions cannot exceed your taxable income for the year.
- The maximum allowable Section 179 deduction is $500,000.
- Investments in equipment in excess of $2 million reduce the $500,000 limit.

The Harris' decided to make the election since their business qualifies for Section 179 deduction. Doing this would allow them to receive the maximum deduction. It was in their best interest to go this route as their business was very successful this year and they would be in a higher tax bracket if they didn't.

You can take the Section 179 deductions for tangible business assets below:

- Machinery
- Office Equipment
- Office Supplies
- Home Office Computers and Furniture
- Off-The-Shelf Software
- "Heavy" (SUV)'s business vehicles used over 50%

*The Harris' Section 179 deductions = $21,200, resulting in $6,996 less tax!*

# Hidden Business Deductions: 'Heavy' vehicles

Business owners interested in using the Section 179 bonus depreciation to deduct the cost of a new vehicle the year it is purchased will be disappointed to learn about the "luxury auto limitations."

For passenger vehicles, trucks, and vans (not meeting the guidelines below) that are used more than 50% in a qualified business use, the total deduction for depreciation including all available bonuses is limited to$ 11,060 for cars and $11,160 for trucks and vans, However, if you are looking for a much larger deduction the first year, consider the "Heavy Vehicle" loophole, discussed in more detail below.

There are two methods for deducting business related expenses for a vehicle: the actual expense (tires, oil, gas, repairs etc) or the standard mileage allowance. By choosing to deduct actual business expenses instead of the standard mileage allowance business owners should note that they can take advantage of owning "heavy" SUVs, vans and pickups. "Heavy" vehicles used more than 50% for business are permitted to be depreciated much faster than passenger vehicles. To classify as a "heavy" vehicle the vehicle purchased for business purposes must have a minimum gross vehicle weight rating (GVWR) of 6,000 pounds. You can deduct up to $25,000 in the first year on  sport utility vehicles (SUVs) as long as the vehicle (new or used) is purchased by December 31st.

This benefit is exclusively for those deducting the "Actual Expenses" for their business vehicle(s).

**Tax Savings Opportunity #3:**

The Harris's purchased a qualified heavy vehicle in 2011 for $58,000 and uses it 85 percent for their business. They used the actual expense method to maximize tax savings by claiming the full depreciation deduction in year one. They can now claim two first-year depreciation deductions for their SUV:

- A Section 179 deduction of up to $25,000 and
- Regular first-year depreciation on the depreciable cost left after the Section 179 deduction.

Tax basis is $49,300 (85 percent of $58,000).
Deductions break down:

| | |
|---|---|
| SUV Tax basis: | $49,300 |
| Section 179 deduction (First Year Write Off): | $25,000 |
| Bonus Depreciation deduction (First Year): (100 percent of $24,300 balance) | $24,300 |
| Normal First Year Depreciation: | $0 |
| Total First Year Savings: | $49,300 |
| Tax Savings – SUV: (Tax Rate 33% * $49,300) | $16,269 |
| Total SUV Cost: (Purchase price $58,000 - tax savings of $16,269) | $41,731 |

Please note for qualified property placed in service from Sept. 9, 2010, through Dec. 31, 2011, there is an additional bonus depreciation tax break. The bonus tax break has been increased from 50% to 100% of the remaining balance. This is another benefit available for those choosing to deduct actual expenses over the standard expense method.

Heavy SUV deductions = $49,300.

By comparison, the first-year depreciation write-off for a new $50,000 sedan used 100% for business would have been only $11,060!

**Total Section 179 deductions= $70,500. ($21,200 +$49,300)**
**Total Section 179 Tax Savings= $24,675 ($7,420 +$17,255)**

# Hidden Business Deductions: Start-Up and Organizational Costs

Business startup costs are the fixed and operating costs acquired before a business owner begins operations. Start-Up and Organizational Costs may include any amounts paid in anticipation of the activity actually becoming a business.

Successful business owners, like the Harris', spend countless hours and variable amounts of money to identify the feasibility and profitability of the desired business venture, long before they can ever begin to make any money.

Small business owners are able to deduct as much as $10,000 of their start-up costs in their first year of business. Note that the deduction limit is reduced by one dollar for every dollar that startup cost exceeds $60,000. Any start up cost over $10,000 can be written off over the next 180 months.

### Tax Savings Opportunity #4:

In the case of the Harris', their total startup cost was less than $14,000. They were able to deduct $10,000 in the first year. The additional $4,000 will be written off over the next several years.

**Total Start-Up and Organizational Costs deduction = $10,000.**

## Tax Planning Savings Totals from Hidden Business Deductions:

- Total Home Office deduction = $35,000.
- Total Section 179 deduction = $70,500.
- Total Start-Up and Organizational Costs deduction = $10,000.
- Total Other Hidden Business Deductions = $30,000.

### The Harris Family Total Tax Planning Savings = $145,500

($35,000 + $70,500 + $10,000 + $30,000)= $145,500 Tax Free Income.

Total Annual Income after tax planning savings discussed here is $204,500 ($350,000 - $145,500). There were other tax reducing/ wealth building strategies not discussed that further reduced their tax liability.

Now, you can appreciate the extensive benefit and importance of tax planning. I urge you to schedule a consultation with a tax advisor. We at TAX ROOF, LLC can utilize your Hidden Business Deductions with powerful tax reducing strategies to reduce your tax liability IMMEDIATELY!

Business owners and Independent contractors, save more on their taxes over a year or two than they spend on the cost of their personalized proactive tax plan. Plus, they have the assurance of knowing that their strategies are aligned with the IRS recommendations. It does not matter how much you earn before tax. How much you owe and ultimately pay in taxes to the IRS depends upon the strategy you implement beforehand. A good tax plan can mean less of your income is taxable. Plus, the deductions and exemptions available to you can be increased significantly. The end result is a lower tax liability and lower taxes paid out of your income.

There are many types of expenses that are deductible for a business. Their deductibility depends on clever tax strategies. Stop losing money!

Visit us today online at www.TAXROOF.com for a **"Free Confidential Tax Analysis."**

*We will investigate your business and reveal your Tax Planning Savings $$.*

# Discover Other Hidden Business Deductions

Here are some additional deductions that many business owners miss in tax savings due to Failure to get a Tax Plan.

- Advertising (internet and newspapers)
- Banking fees
- Dues to professional groups, trade associations and chambers of commerce
- Interest on borrowing (credit cards and loans used to finance business purchases)
- Leasing costs for equipment
- Merchant authorization fees for credit card payments
- Moving equipment and machinery
- Rent for office and other business related space
- Shipping and postage (stamps, other mailing costs, and the cost of renting post-office boxes are deductible)
- Storage and warehousing
- Subscriptions (magazines, newspapers, and trade publications)
- Telephone (additional charges on first home line, business long-distance calls, call forwarding and caller identity, cost of second line and dedicated fax line)
- Cell phone (monthly charges)
- Transportation and Delivery cost of equipment or goods
- Legal and Professional fees (Tax Planning Fees, attorney or document preparation service to prepare the initial paperwork for your business, Specialist, professionals or consultants)
- Business structure setup (cost of forming a corporation).
- Filing fees (costs paid to the state and local agencies for the privilege of doing business and include business licenses, state filing fees, fees for lists of directors, and others).
- Accounting, Tax Preparation (business returns) and bookkeeper fees
- Office equipment (computers, scanners, printers, copiers, fax machine)
- Office furniture (desk, tables, chairs, filing cabinets, as well as art you hang on the walls)

- Office set-up costs (stationery, business cards, logo design)
- Education expenses (related to your current business, trade or occupation)
- ATM Fees, Credit-Card Fees (you can deduct ATM fees, credit-card fees, and other bank charges incurred on your business accounts)
- Books, Magazines, and Newspapers-(business-related books)
- Business Cards (deduct the cost of business cards for yourself and your employees)
- Cleaning Service (the cost of a cleaner, maid service or janitor to maintain your place of work)
- Coffee and Snacks
- Uniforms
- Cost of meals provided to employees (only deducted if there's a business reason for having them eat at work)
- Company Parties (deduct the entire cost of a party where all employees are invited)
- Business entertainment or events that are thrown to promote the business (50% deductible)
- Disabled Access (small businesses can get credits and deductions for the cost of making their place of business accessible to people with disabilities)
- Garbage Pickup (if you pay to have your trash hauled to landfills)
- Greeting Cards (to clients and prospects)
- Lists (if you buy or rent lists of e-mail addresses, mailing addresses, or phone numbers)
- Parking and Tolls (business-related parking costs beyond what you pay to park at your regular place of work are deductible, including tolls paid during business travel.)
- Seminars, Classes, Education and Training- (Employers can fully deduct the cost of job-related education for their workers. Education that improves your knowledge and skills in your current business is deductible, but training for an unrelated trade is not)

- Transportation (If you work primarily out of your home, you can typically write off the transportation expense of getting to and from your clients' places of business and other business-related transportation costs.)
- Internet service provider fees or broadband costs such as high speed cable connections. (BUP of total usage)
- Trade Shows- (entrance fee, conferences, and other industry meetings)
- Web site (you can deduct hosting fees, domain cost, wed development and web design costs.)
- Security Systems (the business cost of security devices, installation and monitoring fees for the entire protected area (normally the entire home)
- Plus many more!

### <u>How Much Money Are You Losing<br>in Missed Business Deductions?</u>

Total $_____ Tax Free Income Lost<br>from the #1 Tax Mistake: Failure to Plan!

# Dionne Joseph Thomas, MBA, PMP, EA, CTC

Email: Info@taxroof.com
Phone: 623.374.6455
Fax: 623.374.6562

Website: http://www.taxroof.com

My name is Dionne Joseph Thomas and I am NOT your typical "Tax Professional."

Over the course of my professional career I have graduated with a Masters in Marketing specializing in Strategic Planning and combined it with the Project Management Professional Certification (PMP) to become a Project Management Dynamo.

I once started a business without consulting a tax planning professional and I was audited after submitting my very first tax return. As overwhelming as that experience is to a new business owner, I am not the type of person that gives up quickly. My husband and I are meticulous with our record keeping and we did a lot of research to prepare ourselves to face the IRS. We represented ourselves to the IRS and were able to successfully prove our case to their satisfaction. During the course of this ordeal I discovered a few tax planning strategies that could have prevented the experience entirely. It also taught me that I was paying entirely too much in taxes, and, had I implemented some of the strategies I learnt at the beginning, my tax liability would have been even less. This fueled the desire within me to know everything about taxes. I spent the next few years studying everything I could about taxation, and applied my knowledge of strategic planning to find the ways to LEGALLY reduce one's tax liability. I have since used this knowledge to help myself and others.

I focused on IRS approved strategies to assist both business owners(start up or established) and independent contractors. This further motivated my husband and I to gain our certification as Enrolled Agents (EA) and me to become a Certified Tax Coach (CTC). I founded TAX ROOF, LLC to assist our clients to utilize proactive tax planning strategies and to provide personalized business solutions that ensure our clients enjoy substantial savings year after year.

TAX ROOF, LLC is an environmentally conscious family owned firm where "Quality," "Integrity," and "Personalized Service" are our core values. Our personalized business solutions also provide our startup business clients with a one stop shop for their business needs. Our Tax Team of Enrolled Agents are year round tax professionals who specialize in proactive tax planning strategies. We collaborate on every case individually to create personalized tax plans that take advantage of every legal deduction, credit loophole and strategy available for our clients to enjoy the maximum possible tax savings!

We also provide Free Tax Analysis to determine how much money we can save you in taxes before you commit to anything.

Visit us today online at www.taxroof.com or email us at info@taxroof.com for your "Free Tax Analysis."

All Tax Planning sessions are by Appointment Only.

Thank you for the opportunity to serve you.

# CHAPTER TWELVE

# Wacky Tax Deductions

## By Larisa Humphrey, CTC

Ever thought of writing off sex with prostitutes on your taxes?

Believe it or not, one New York attorney claimed $65,934 in prostitute services as a medical expense. I guess this legal eagle overlooked the fact that prostitution is illegal and you cannot deduct anything illegal on your tax returns.

What was he thinking while presenting his detailed journal documenting each visit with prostitutes to the tax court? Since these "services" were illegal, the tax court ruled that they were not deductible. The court also disallowed $5,000 for pornography & sex therapy books and magazines, saying "those amounts were incurred for the petitioner's general welfare, not pursuant to a doctor's prescription or for a specific medical condition."

I guess when it comes to tax deductions, many taxpayers don't seem to think the legality of the matter, matters. This is apparently the situation in the case of a Pittsburgh furniture store owner who had been trying to sell his business for years with no luck.

He finally hired someone to burn the store down & collected $500,000 from his insurance company. The final nail in his coffin was claiming the $10,000 he paid the arsonist as a "consulting fee" on his taxes. He was audited two years later and in addition to the owner receiving a $6,500 penalty, both men ended up in prison.

Would you believe the IRS grants tax deductions paid because of the commission of a crime? A dentist's wife kept his books and, unbeknownst to him, billed insurance companies for services he didn't perform. After her scheme was uncovered, she was sentenced to 18 months in jail, but she wasn't required to pay restitution. The dentist repaid the ill-gotten gains to settle the insurer's civil claims against his practice. Since the repayment merely compensated the insurer for its loss and wasn't punitive, the dentist was allowed to deduct it as a business expense. In fact, the loss created by the write-off triggered a refund of taxes paid in prior years.

Then there is good-time-Charlie who drank too much at a party, but had the good sense to arrange a ride home. A few hours later, after slowing down in his revelry, he thought he was okay to drive. But his car slid off the road and rolled over. He was arrested for drunken driving because his blood alcohol reading was over the legal limit. His insurance company refused to pay for the damage to his car because of the arrest. But the Tax Court let him deduct the cost of the damage as a casualty loss because it said that he had "tried to act reasonably." Had he driven straight home from the party with a high blood alcohol level and had the accident, the court declared that it would have nixed his deduction because his actions would have constituted gross negligence.

Not all "unusual" tax deductions are associated with breaking the law.

Let's take for instance, the case of a 65-year-old Kissimmee, FL woman who liked her 20-something student renter/handyman so much that she deemed him "nephew" and claimed him as a dependent on her taxes. The IRS caught on three years later, and slapped her with $5,000 in back taxes and a $2,000 penalty.

Then there was a gas station owner who ended up in tax court after deducting the free beer he gave his customers as a business expense.

(Hope they didn't drink it until they got home!) The court ruled the beer was a legitimate expense and upheld the deduction. But when an Oklahoma businessman tried to deduct several cases of whiskey he gave to his clients as an "entertainment expense" his deduction was denied.

Speaking of drinks, some people really know how to "milk" the system. The owners of a dairy business went on an African safari and wrote it off as a business expense. Justification for the deduction was "many of the dairy's promotional activities and marketing efforts included wild animals." (Wild dairy cows?) The IRS agreed and upheld the trip as an "ordinary & necessary" deduction.

An airline pilot and a massage therapist moved their mobile home to a 78-acre lot in Tennessee and bought two emus and twenty chickens. (No...this is not the start of a corny joke, it's an actual tax deduction claim!) From "time to time," the couple would sell chicken eggs (for $1 a dozen) and emu feathers. They claimed the cost of the animal's feed and maintenance as a business expense on their taxes. Since they didn't record the income generated from the animals, the tax court ruled this was not a legitimate business and disallowed the deductions.

Another pilot (is there something that affects you while flying?) attempted to deduct loofa sponges as business expenses. What was his business? Aviation. He also claimed grass seed, a shower curtain & sporting goods as business expenses. The Tax Court deemed these items personal and not necessary for his job as a pilot.

A Massachusetts doctor wrote off thousands of dollars in costs for donating sperm to in vitro fertilization. The Tax Court denied this deduction saying these donations didn't affect his health and were not legitimate medical expenses. The court said since he had no physical or mental defect or illness which prohibited him from procreating naturally...the petitioner's choice to undertake these procedures was an entirely personal/non-medical decision.

I guess if you are donating sperm you feel like you deserve some type of tax deduction reward for your efforts. There's a Manhattan man who tried to take a "depletion allowance" for sperm donations he had made throughout the year. Of course, this was also disallowed.

One of rock star Rod Stewart's professional musicians claimed his underwear as a deduction on his taxes. (Well hey...if you think you're sexy...) He also wrote off his silk boxers, leather pants, hat & vest. Tax court actually allowed the flashy outer garments, but to the underwear, they said no.

After a doctor suggested dancing would be good for her arthritis-plagued hips, an 85-year-old Arizona woman deducted more than $8,000 for dance lessons on her taxes. Since that went off without a hitch, the following year, she had receipts for more than $35,000 in dance lessons and $18,000 in gowns and cruises for her and her 20-something dance instructor. Unfortunately, the client died before the investigation was finished.

A Wisconsin body builder claimed over $4,000 in buffalo meat, posing oil and protein shakes as business expenses. He said he ate three pounds of buffalo meat a day, all year long, for muscle development since "it has more protein than other meats." The tax court disallowed the meat since it could be eaten by anyone and called it a personal expense. But the oils & tanning products were allowed, including a specific brand that was marketed only through professional body building magazines, which he applied to his skin to "enhance his appearance."

The IRS actually upheld the purr-fect solution to a nasty rat & snake problem. A clever junkyard owner set out bowls of pet food each night to attract wild cats. Not only did our feline friends eat the cat food, they also feasted on the unwanted guests. Since the cats helped make the business safer for customers, the pet food was allowed as a deduction.

Millions of dogs are left at home alone everyday while their owners go off to work. I guess this pooch's owner felt his puppy was more distressed than most so he hired a sitter to come in and watch his dog everyday. The IRS just didn't take too kindly to the taxpayer deducting the cost using the child care credit which is intended for children & legal dependents. Unfortunately, pets do not qualify. Deduction denied.

Did you know that certain types of cosmetic surgery may be a legitimate tax write-off if you can show that it is a necessity for your job? Take the case of exotic dancer Cynthia Hess (a.k.a. "Chesty Love"), who sued the IRS in order to take a $2,088 tax deduction for her breast augmentation, resulting in size 56FF chest. She was allowed to take the tax write-off because her 20 pound breasts were used for the purposes of making money at an Indiana strip club, and were essentially viewed as a "stage prop."

What about the Texas rancher who attended his first tax audit along with his CPA. When the rancher's tax depreciation schedule listed 15-20 animals as breeding stock, the no-nonsense young IRS agent challenged the old cowboy. "I presume you breed these animals?" she asked pointedly. Without hesitation, the rancher replied, "Nope," sending his CPA into mild tachycardia. After a sufficient pause, the rancher finished the popular Texas joke, "I've got a bull for that."

Here are a few of the more "creative" tax deductions:

- One couple claimed that a $2,500 mink coat was an ordinary & necessary business expense needed for public relations and advertising, since the wife must dress well to "impress" potential clients. The Tax Court denied the claim.

- An actor tried to take a business deduction for dentures because he claimed they enabled him to "enunciate without a hiss." Deduction denied. In another case, a man claimed his dentures as a deduction on his taxes because they fell into the toilet, which he claimed was an "act-of-God casualty loss." Again, deduction denied.

- There was a landscaper being audited because he deducted expenses he incurred caring for his dog. He felt the dog was "working" because he would pull the wagon on landscaping jobs. Claim denied.

- The IRS approved a parent's write-off of her son's clarinet lessons as a medical expense. The parent claimed and the orthodontist confirmed that playing the instrument was correcting the child's overbite. The IRS agreed.

- A Texas lady donated $40,000 to charity which was almost as much as her income. She had gone through a divorce after her cheating ex-husband left her and donated his portion of the household items (including 3 sets of golf clubs) to Goodwill. Since her charitable contribution was limited to 50% of her adjusted gross income, she wound up with right around $15,000 in charitable contributions.

- A deduction for the cost of boarding school as medical expense for another taxpayer was allowed, because their child had respiratory problems.
- Organic food was allowed as a medical expense because the taxpayer had only claimed the price difference between organic and regular, chemically treated food.
- Milk and nail polish remover were not considered deductible as a business expense for a person employed as a tax preparer.
- A fallout shelter, claimed as preventive medicine, was denied.
- Another taxpayer tried unsuccessfully to deduct dancing lessons as a medical expense to improve varicose veins.
- An Ohio woman tried to write off her tricked-out hot tub for medical reasons. A portion of it was deductible, but the in-tub stereo, underwater speakers and mood lighting were not included.
- A Texas woman didn't like the mature trees in her yard so she dug them up and donated them to charity. She had to get an appraiser to value the trees, and the IRS allowed the deduction.
- One Arizona man wanted a home office deduction for the toilet paper he bought for his home. Wonder what the nature of his business was?
- Another taxpayer tried to sneak in a check for over $2000 written to a gynecologist. It was classified on his business books as "repairs & maintenance."
- Then there's a taxpayer who tried to write off a $100,000 swimming pool for medical reasons, because "swimming, relaxed him so he could earn more money, which in turn would be taxable." Un-swimmingly, this deduction was denied.
- A man who felt he was a woman trapped in a male body was diagnosed with gender-identity disorder. This transgender taxpayer claimed almost $22,000 in out-of-pocket medical costs for multiple surgeries, including hormone therapy, sexual-reassignment surgeries and breast augmentation, in order to become a woman. The tax court ruled that the costs of the

hormone therapy and the sex-change operation — a total of $14,500 — qualified as deductible medical expenses because those procedures helped treat the disease. But the court nixed the deduction for the cost of breast augmentation, saying that was nondeductible cosmetic surgery.

- A man hired his live-in girlfriend to manage several of his rental properties. Her duties included finding furniture, overseeing repairs and running his personal household. The Tax Court let him deduct as a business expense $2,500 of the $9,000 he paid her but disallowed the cost of her housekeeping chores as nondeductible personal services.

- Rather than drive five to seven hours to check on their rental condo or be tied to the only daily commercial flight available, a couple bought their own plane. The Tax Court allowed them to deduct their condo-related trips on the aircraft, including the cost of fuel and depreciation for the portion of time used for business-related purposes, even though these costs increased their overall rental loss on the condo.

- And don't forget the Amish man who pimped out his buggy with velvet interior, dash lights, kick plates, tinted windshield, speedometer, hydraulic brakes & dimmer switches, fuzzy dice & boom boxes. He was able to write off the buggy because it was used for business, but all the extras were not deductible.

As you can see, American taxpayers are full of creativity when it comes to tax deductions. My advice is to check with a Certified Tax Coach to make sure your "deductions" are legal so you won't lose in tax court or even worse, be slapped with a big fine or a lengthy prison sentence.

# Larisa Humphrey, CTC

I started Abundant Returns Tax Service back in 1991 after seeing on TV that Ross Perot, then presidential candidate and CEO of a multi-billion dollar corporation, **paid less than $2000 in personal income taxes!**

I just couldn't believe it because **I made $35,000 that year and paid More Than $4000 in federal taxes alone!!!** I paid more than double the taxes a Billionaire paid!!!

I was flabbergasted to say the least. "He's a billionaire," I kept saying to myself. "How is it legal for me to pay more taxes than a billionaire?"

I kept tossing it around in my head. I just couldn't believe it. I worried about how I was going to pay the rent. I struggled to buy a bus pass every week. I had to make "arrangements" every month to pay my utility bills. My grocery budget was $15/week and I was paying more income taxes than a billionaire?!!!

It made absolutely no sense to me. It still makes no sense to me...20 years later! (If I think about it long enough, I still get mad.)

This was an "a-ha" moment for me—a life lesson that shattered my very sheltered view of reality. I learned two very valuable lessons—life is not fair and rich people can avoid income taxes.

So I got busy.

I took several income tax preparation courses. I read hundreds of books on taxes. I've prepared thousands of tax returns.

I worked for the IRS and a local tax office. I learned about taxes and how to use the tax law to my advantage. I learned how to live "tax free" like billionaires do.

Now I'm ready to share that knowledge with you so you can "Keep More Money In Your Pocket" too. In my ebook, "Pay Yourself Instead of Uncle Sam," I explore many tax strategies that will help you reduce your taxes as low as possible. You can find it at www.find-business-tax-deductions.com.

You can contact me at larisa@abundantreturns.com or feel free to give me a call at 770-451-6330.

# CHAPTER THIRTEEN

# Match.com
# For Accountants

## BY JOHN POLLOCK, CWS CTC

Looking for a perfect partner whether in life or business is always daunting. I hope to take the mystery out of it because I am just like you. Well, not exactly like you, but I had to find the right CPA and tax advisor just like you.

Before helping you on your journey toward true love, or true like, at least, I would like to explain how I am like you.

Before I partnered with Larry Patterson, CPA, to build one of the largest CPA firms in Dallas, and before I became a Certified Tax Coach I was, and still am, a financial advisor, I owned John Pollock, Inc. an Insurance and Financial Planning Firm and Pollock Advisory Group, Inc. a Registered Investment Advisory firm. I had built these firms into a robust and successful practice and knew that I needed to integrate tax planning into my overall business plan in order to effectively serve my clients. I suspect you are similar in that you know that you need proactive tax planning in your life, otherwise you wouldn't have this book in your hands. In order to kick-start my "tax planning"service, I offered a cheap tax return preparation service. After a few years of this disaster, I knew I had to alter my business. The "take away" from my experience is that I really should not have been in a professional discipline without a partner that knew what they were doing in that business. Regardless of my competence in my other firms, the tax code is exceptionally complex and it can't be solved by throwing software and people at it. You have to work with a pro, someone that lives and breathes the tax code, and someone that not only has the knowledge, but also the experience on how to apply it to your life.

I see this same mistake made by other professionals. A doctor thinks he is smart in his profession so he ventures into real estate and then loses money. An engineer who is brilliant in his profession thinks that all he needs is a software package and he can "figure it out." What starts as confidence that was earned in one profession slips into incompetence when applied to a field outside your scope of expertise. Learn from the mistake that took me years to realize, competency in one profession does not transfer to the world of taxes.

I had to start down the journey to find a tax person that I could trust, someone that was good at what I wasn't good at, like accounting and bookkeeping and payroll and most important, helping me pay the least amount of taxes. This is an example of where my pain is your gain! With that short introduction allow me to help you find the right lifetime mate, or at least a great proactive tax planner.

## Decide you don't want to be single.

At some point in your personal or business life you are going to realize that some things are better done by someone else who is an expert at those things. Therefore, you are going to need a partner. In every 12 step program the first step to recovery is admitting you have a problem and being aware of your limits. You need to know what you don't know. Until you admit that you can't keep up with the tax code and you would rather grow your life or business, instead of recording what you are doing and have done, than you are going to spend a lot of wasted hours on something that can be done better, faster, and cheaper (more economically) than you could do on your own. And admit it, you don't care about the tax code, you just want to pay the least amount the code allows, and unless you have a chronic case of insomnia, tackling the tax code in the evenings is not a good use of your time or energy, so LET GO. I have heard there are lots of studies that say married people are happier than single people, I can't comment on that, but I can say that those people that have a proactive tax advisor, that has saved them money on taxes, are much happier than people paying higher taxes with their current accountant, tax preparer or CPA, I don't have a study, however I am comfortable stating it as fact.

# Start dating!

I have repeatedly explained to my kids that the purpose of dating is to find or eliminate a potential spouse. (Do they really need to have a boyfriend at 11, really!? But I digress.) Finding the right Proactive Tax Advisor is similar to dating, but not nearly as fun and rarely involves dinner and a movie. But it is important, in that you are going to develop a relationship that will span many years and they will know details about you. They will know more about your money than many spouses, you will be sharing information very few people know. So it is important you get it right. Before our CPA firm Patterson and Pollock, LLC, was founded, I had to make sure I found a partner that I was willing to do some scary stuff with, like buying a million dollar CPA firm together. Your choice may not have quite the financial ramifications as mine, but it does have both financially rewarding and/or detrimental consequences. So you have been on lots of "dates" how do you know you have found "the one" in a matter where there aren't emotions and physical attraction?

# Are they like you?

In matters of the heart you want to find someone that you have something in common with, right? The same hopes , dreams, religion, desire for kids; something that leads you to believe this is the one. You want someone that "gets you," is "on the same page." What you are looking for is someone that is *PHILOSOPHICALLY ALIGNED.* Finding a Proactive Tax Planner is similar; allow me to explain using a case that came into my office. The gentlemen, we will call Fred, had a successful business in the construction field. He was frustrated because his CPA would not use his mortgage interest as a tax write off. His explanation was that someone with Fred's level of success should pay his "fair share."

I told Fred that his fair share is whatever the law legally required and it was completely fair to write off his mortgage interest just like everyone in the United States. I found thousands of dollars in additional tax reduction strategies that his former (you knew that was coming) CPA was unwilling to use.

In this case, Fred's former accountant was not philosophically aligned with Fred's beliefs. Fred believes in taking advantage of every available break, while his old accountant believes Fred should pay his "fair share." Just like a marriage with differing beliefs is difficult, partnering with an advisor with differing beliefs is a recipe for disaster!

If you own and operate a business you are an entrepreneur. You need to find a Proactive Tax Planner that thinks like an entrepreneur. Basically you want an entrepreneur in the tax and accounting business, not a just an accountant. This may seem like a confusing or subtle distinction, but it is critical, you want someone that wants you to keep more of your money as much as you do. You want someone that is on the same page and philosophically aligned.

You would think this would be easy to find, IT ISN'T! I met 10 different CPA's over 2 years before I met Larry. I laid out a business plan that grew our businesses in parallel and was almost entirely funded by me, and run by him, yet I could not find a CPA that "got it." When I showed my idea to my current business partner for the first time he looked at me perplexed and said, "why wouldn't I want to do this?" He "got it," and the partnership began. This will happen with you too, you will meet the person that gets it, and wants to work with you and toward your mutual success. Be patient, they are out there, of course you can just look for someone that has the CTC initials behind their name (Certified Tax Coach's are all entrepreneurs, or they would not be attracted to this premier designation).

# Don't be cheap!

I understand cheap, my mom washed straws, insisted on cloth napkins and never use paper plates or plastic cups, and this was way before Going Green was in vogue. There is a great quote from Paul Neal "Red" Adair the famous oil fire fighter, "If you think it's expensive to hire a professional to do the job, wait until you hire an amateur."

There is not a man alive, when he was actively pursuing his future spouse, that thought, "how can I convince her to marry me, without spending any money?" OK, maybe some guy did, but not many. Good relationships cost money, there is no getting around it, if you want someone good in any field of endeavor you are going to have to pay for it. The old cliché "you get what you pay for" is especially true in the area of business and financial planning. If I could save you $5,000 each year, every year, with a good tax plan, how much would that money be worth to you? Would you search for a discount? What part of the $5,000 lower tax bill would you be willing to do without in order to gain a discount?

It's important to be smart. A guy that cheats on a girl while dating, treats her with disrespect while buying her a 10 carat ring, is still a bad choice. In love you still need to use your head. In business you are looking for value. Ask yourself would you pay $1,500 now to save $5,000 every year? Most would say yes to this. But the choice is usually more complicated. The choice most taxpayers usually make is to buy a $50 software package and do their own taxes rather than pay someone a few hundred dollars for them to do it. Both choices appear equal, but when you make the decision, you buy the cheaper software.

Inevitably when you make the commodity decision, you get what you pay for, and there are negative consequences. Perhaps you receive a notice from the IRS that your taxes are missing five different items. You ignored two of them because you read the form wrong. Another two were misinterpretations and were, in fact, something else. Finally, you had a sale that you knew had no tax but the IRS disagreed. I recently helped a client with a similar situation. I had to track down all the appropriate forms and paperwork. This took hours of his time and my time. His bill included unnecessary charges by my firm in addition to tax penalties and interest. So far his $50 software has cost him thousands of dollars. In what complex field of endeavor have you been able to get it right on the first try? Do you think tax counts as a complex field of endeavor? Do you think you can get it right?

Just like Paul Neal "Red" Adair says, amateurs are expensive, especially if the amateur is you.

# Be Proactive

You have decided you don't want to be alone in the tax jungle, you have decided to spend money on a good trail guide and good tools like a tax machete. You have interviewed and found the guide through the jungle, now you are ready to settle down. Do you just move in and wait to see what happens? NO! Unfortunately this is what most CPA's do, they wait till the year is over and they see what you have done and they react to try and fix it. In most cases it is like squeezing toothpaste out of a tube, once the toothpaste is out it isn't going back in.

This is a typical conversation:

**CPA:** So I have notice that you did X last year.
**You:** Yeah, is that bad?
**CPA:** Yes, you shouldn't have done that, it'll cost you.
**You:** OK?! What should I do different next year?
**CPA:** I don't know just don't do X again.

When I repeat this dialogue in my office I get the tongue in cheek response from clients, "Did you bug my CPA's office?" This is reactive planning; this whole book is about proactive planning. When was the last time your accountant gave you an idea, in advance, that changed the way you did business so that you could reduce your taxes?

Make sure you develop a plan that proactively pursues tax reduction (within the legal confines of the law, of course). The advantage of working with accountants is that the record keeping necessary to implement a proactive tax plan is too complicated and cumbersome for mere mortals like you and me. But for accountants it is easy, implementation of complex accounting is fun for them.

On the other hand, many accountants are terrible at forward thinking. They are great at the above mentioned "compliance" work, and they are great at recording history but they are terrible at forward thinking, planning to write history. This is why you are looking for an entrepreneur, they are naturally forward thinking problem solvers, you combine that with the analytical mind that has studied the tax code and someone who applies these laws proactively, what you get appears to be magic.

Once a plan is in place typically there isn't a need for drastic changes, but there may be a need for course corrections. An example is like a cruise from New York to England, you know the exact direction of the destination but depending on the currents and winds you may need to course-correct. A proactive advisor will help with this. The only thing that may change your destination is that you find out there are riots in England and the boat can't dock. So what would change a Proactive Tax Plan? A change in the tax code or a change in the circumstances of ones personal life situation, and since that rarely happens... Oh wait, on the other hand make sure you work with someone that watches the tax code like a hawk and/or whenever congress is in session.

# Like that lasts a lifetime

Love should be reserved for matters of the heart. But, a deep, substantial like can exist for someone that saves you thousands of dollars in taxes. Now you know what to look for:

- Someone that does for you what you can't do for yourself.
- Someone that is philosophically aligned with your objective of helping you keep the money you earned.
- Someone that is looking ahead at taxes so you can focus on being the best you can be on your journey.
- Someone that you are happy to pay what they are worth, because they add value to the relationship.

That is the recipe for true like!

# John Pollock

John Pollock is currently the President of Pollock Advisory Group, Inc., a Registered Investment Advisory firm, John Pollock, Inc. an insurance, estate and legacy planning firm and is a principle of Patterson & Pollock, LLC, a Certified Public Accounting firm that specializes in lowering taxes and increasing profits for small businesses. John began his career on the corporate side of financial  services working with CFO's of major corporations helping them to manage cash flow and account receivables more effectively and cost efficiently. This corporate experience gives John a perspective and experience that is not typically found in the financial services industry.

John's goal is to help his clients design a plan that allows them to build and preserve a life and legacy of meaning. He has presented to hundreds of audiences live and on his radio show, his trademarked concepts of Investor Peace™, Financial Gravity™, the Diversity Trinity™, Segmenting, Cash Flow Equivalent Return™ and Timeless Wisdom, Strategic Application™. These tested and consistently effective concepts came from a compilation of his past business experience and the years of working with and customizing plans for his clients.

John's relentless pursuit of excellence has earned him several industry initials and designations, the two he believes have the greatest impact on his ability to serve his clients are, Certified Tax Coach (CTC) and Certified Wealth Strategist (CWS)

John shares his life with his wife Krista and his four kids, Tyler, Ansley, Emily and Alyssa in Allen, Texas.

www.johnpollockfinancial.com

# CHAPTER FOURTEEN

# Winning The Game Without Breaking The Rules

By Ronald D'Arminio, CPA CTC

*"I am proud to be paying taxes in the United States. The only thing is — I could be just as proud for half the money."*
—**Arthur Godfrey**, entertainer, as reported on IRS.gov

## Electing How Your Business is Taxed

Throughout this book you have been introduced to several tax planning opportunities that as the title states are often overlooked. Furthermore, you have been introduced to several advanced tax strategies and concepts that you can pick and choose which make sense for your facts and circumstances.

Chapter Four reveals that owning your own business is one of the last legal tax shelters still available to every taxpayer. Chapter Six, To LLC or Not to LLC?, takes you through an in depth look at the different types of entities that you can use to operate your business or rental activities. The rest of this book is devoted to applying tax strategies among those different entities. What does it all mean? At this point you're probably considering many of these ideas and confused about where to start? I would suggest you consider two fundamental tax concepts when starting your new business or restructuring your existing business.

**The way your business is ORGANIZED and the way it ELECTS to be TAXED can save you thousands each year.**

Let's look at how these concepts can be applied to a practical situation. When I first met with Victor, he was like most successful business owners. He was an aggressive entrepreneur who built his manufacturing business from the ground up. Like most business owners, he relied on a CPA to advise him and prepare his tax returns. He had every reason to believe he was taking advantage of every tax break afforded to small business owners like him under the Internal Revenue Code. But we learned in Chapter Thirteen, Match.com For Accountants, that not all CPAs or tax preparers are the same. Victor eventually learned he had been overpaying thousands of dollars in taxes each year.

Victor, like so many start-up business owners, was operating as a single member LLC. Each year his accountant prepared a schedule C for his business and included it as a part of his individual tax return.

I can hear your questions already. So what's wrong with that? After all, an LLC is probably the easiest and cheapest entity to set up that provides liability protection at the entity level. I don't have to pay any federal taxes at the entity level. Most states don't tax LLCs and most states have a relatively low annual fee compared to corporate annual fees and minimum taxes.

Is it possible that the same amount of taxable income from the same business operations can result in two different tax liabilities, just because I'm an LLC versus an S Corp? Yes.

Let's compare what happens when we take the same business and the same income in a single member LLC and in an S Corporation. By default the LLC is taxed as a disregarded entity on Form 1040, schedule C. On the other hand, a corporation with a sole shareholder that elects to be taxed as an S Corporation is treated differently. Let's use a $100,000 net income where $52,000 is taken as a reasonable compensation throughout the year and the remaining $48,000 is taken as a profit distribution at the end of the year. As you can see from the chart below, Social Security and Medicare taxes are paid on the $52,000 in salary but the remaining profit on the LLC is subject to additional self employment taxes that the S corporation profit is not subject to. Maybe an LLC is not so cheap to operate after all, and maybe the additional administrative costs of an S corporation are not beginning to look so bad.

| $100,000 of Total Business Earnings from a single-member LLC taxed as a Sole Proprietorship | | $100,000 of Total Business Earnings from a Corporation electing to be taxed as an S Corporation | |
|---|---|---|---|
| SE Income | $100,000 | Salary | $ 52,000 |
| SE Tax | $ 14,130 | FICA | $ 7,956 |
| Net | $ 85,870 | Net | $ 92,044 |

\* SE Tax and FICA were calculated using a combined 15.3% employer and employee rate

In the above example, a business owner would keep $6,174 more in his or her pocket every year by electing to be taxed as an S Corporation. There are no self-employment nor FICA taxes applied to the remaining $48,000 of earnings received as a pass-through from the S Corporation.

> *"As a citizen, you have an obligation to the country's tax system, but you also have an obligation to yourself to know your rights under the law and possible tax deductions — and to claim every one of them."*

—Donald Alexander, Former IRS Commissioner

# Avoiding an Audit

In my 27 years of experience, I have met with business owners from all walks of life that have spanned a spectrum of business industries. Two things they all have in common when it comes to income taxes are (1) they all want to pay as little tax as possible but (2) they do not want to do anything to trigger an IRS audit. It's a common misconception that taking advantage of tax planning strategies may result in a greater risk of being audited. Granted you must have a bona fide business purpose for either restructuring your business or using multiple entities.

Let's take our example of using an S corporation to eliminate $6,174 in self-employment taxes. You may have thought, this sounds great, but if I elect to be taxed as an S corporation in order to save taxes my odds of being audited will be much higher than if I continue to report my business income and deductions on schedule C. Not true, but don't take my word for it, let's look at actual statistical data from the IRS. Each year the IRS publishes a Data Book. The most recent IRS Data Book includes information on tax returns that were filed in calendar year 2009 and were examined in fiscal year 2010. The IRS examined almost 1 percent of all tax returns filed in calendar year 2009 but how that overall audit rate breaks down among individual tax returns and business tax returns provides a realistic picture of true audit risk. I've included a chart that highlights the different audit rates on the next page. Overall 1.1 percent of individual tax returns that were filed in calendar year 2009 were audited in fiscal year 2010. For individual returns with total positive income under $200,000 the rate dropped to 0.5 percent but if that same return included a Schedule E (Supplemental Income and Loss), Form 2106 (Employee Business Expenses) or Schedule C with gross receipts under $25,000, the audit rate jumped to 1.2%. For schedule Cs with gross receipts between $25,000 and $100,000 the audit rate more than doubled to 2.5%; Schedule C with gross receipts between $100,000 and $200,000 4.7% and those with gross receipts of $200,000 or more 3.3%. For C Corporations filing Form 1120 the overall audit rate was 1.4% and that dropped down to 0.9% for small corporations, which are corporate returns filed with assets less than $10 million. The returns that had the lowest overall audit rate—partnerships and S Corporations each with a 0.4% audit rate.

| Return Type | Returns Filed | Returns Examined | Audit % |
|---|---|---|---|
| All Returns | 187,124,450 | 1,735,083 | 0.9 |
| Individual Returns (Form 1040) | 142,823,105 | 1,581,394 | 1.1 |
| with total positive income under $200,000 without Schedules C, E or Form 2106 | 80,254,935 | 363,424 | 0.5 |
| with Schedule E or Form 2106 | 16,052,553 | 190,746 | 1.2 |
| Schedule C (by Gross Receipts) | | | |
| Under $25,000 | 10,736,434 | 132,584 | 1.2 |
| Between $25,000 and $100,000 | 3,136,694 | 79,389 | 2.5 |
| Between $100,000 and $200,000 | 893,707 | 42,403 | 4.7 |
| $200,000 and more | 705,877 | 23,569 | 3.3 |
| C Corporation Returns (Form 1120) | 2,143,808 | 29,803 | 1.4 |
| Small Corporation Returns | 2,041,474 | 19,127 | 0.9 |
| Partnership Returns (Form 1065) | 3,423,583 | 12,406 | 0.4 |
| S Corporation Returns (Form 1120S) | 4,414,662 | 16,327 | 0.4 |

*Plain English Interpretation:* If you operate as an S Corporation your audit risk based on the most recent statistics is less than one half of one percent. Moreover, if you operate a business with gross receipts between $100,000 and $200,000 and are filing a Schedule C you are more than 10 times more likely to be audited. If you are selected for an audit, I'll discuss steps you can take to audit proof your return later in this chapter.

# Passive Activity Rules

*The Beginning:* Early in my professional career there was much talk of a flat tax, tax simplification and fairness. Ultimately the Tax Reform Act of 1986 (TRA 86) was signed into law by President Reagan on October 22, 1986. This Act was a complete overhaul of the prior Internal Revenue Code and created the Internal Revenue Code of 1986. Congress wanted a fairer tax system that wouldn't allow *"high-income individuals to pay far lower rates of tax than other, less affluent individuals."* Does this sound familiar to what we are still hearing 25 years later? Congress also wanted a simpler tax system and believed it achieved this by establishing two individual income tax rates to replace more than a dozen in the previous rate schedules. In addition, increases to the standard deduction were intended to simplify tax return filings by greatly reducing the number of taxpayers who would itemize their deductions. The Tax Reform Act of 1986 did in fact provide for only 15 and 28 percent individual income tax rates, but that's where the simplification ended. The fairness aspect of TRA 86 introduced the Passive Activity Rules we still have today. In order to prevent the use of so called "tax shelters" and achieve what was perceived as fairness, TRA 86 moved away from simplicity and created complexity. The new limitation on passive activity losses contained in the act created more confusion and left so many questions that in 1987 the Joint Committee on Taxation issued the "General Explanation of the Tax Reform Act of 1986." That *general* explanation ended on page One Thousand Three Hundred Fifty Two! The good news is that with proper planning, complexity creates opportunity.

> *"There is nothing wrong with a strategy to avoid the payment of taxes. The Internal Revenue Code doesn't prevent that."*
> —William H. Rehnquist, Chief Justice of the US Supreme Court

# Opportunities Using the Passive Activity Rules

**Background:** A passive activity is any rental activity or trade or business activity that you do not materially participate in. Rental activity by definition is a passive activity unless certain exceptions are met which I'll discuss later. Whether an activity is deemed passive or not determines how net income or losses from that activity can be used for tax purposes. Remember that the ability to deduct losses from passive activities against trade or business income or investment income was considered a tax shelter. When the passive activity rules were first enacted, they were included in a special section of the act. The intent was to limit the ability to deduct losses or claim credits, so if you have a net loss from a passive activity you can only deduct that loss from other passive activity income. Alternately said, you cannot deduct a passive loss from earned income such as wages or income from your trade or business in which you materially participate. If you do not have any passive income, then your passive loss is suspended and carried over to future tax years. When you have a complete disposition of your interest in a passive activity, you may deduct any suspended losses against other income. If you have other passive income in the year of disposition, your suspended losses must be used against passive income first, with any remaining amount being deducted against other non-passive income.

*Material Participation:* If you materially participate in an activity then it is not considered passive. The IRS considers you to materially participate in an activity if you meet at least one of the following six conditions:

- You participate in the activity for more than 500 hours in the year;
- Your participation in the activity constitutes substantially all of the participation in the activity;
- You participate for at least 100 hours during the year and it is more than any other individuals participation;
- You materially participated in any 5 of the preceding 10 years;
- You participated in the activity for any of the preceding 3 years and the activity is a personal service activity;
- You participate in the activity on a regular, continuous and substantial basis.

*Caution:* A limited partner's investment is generally considered passive by nature of the limited liability and limited involvement.

What this means for you is, if you have passive losses, you can only deduct them against passive income. If you currently have suspended passive losses (not deducted on your current tax return) a smart tax strategy will help you look for ways to generate passive income so that you can benefit from the losses.

These passive income opportunities might already exist if you currently own your own business with multiple streams of revenue. Using the rules stated above, it is possible to create a business in which you do not materially participate for purposes of creating passive income. This essentially helps to bring in "tax free" income to the extent that your passive losses effectively eliminate this income on your tax return.

It is true that this is a complex area of the tax code, but it can be a very effective way to reduce your overall tax and make use of the losses you may incur from passive activities including real estate investments. Make sure you are working with an advisor like a Certified Tax Coach who is experienced and familiar with this area of tax planning.

# $25,000 Rental Real Estate Allowance

An exception to limiting your deduction of passive losses against only other passive income is available for $25,000 of passive losses from a rental real estate activity that you actively participate in. This exception allows you to offset up to $25,000 of rental real estate passive losses against your other non-passive income from your business, wages and investments. The IRS defines active participation as participating in management decisions or arranging for others to provide services in a significant and bona fide sense. Therefore, active participation is not as difficult to satisfy when compared to the material participation guidelines. You are not considered to actively participate in an activity if you own less than a 10 percent interest in it at any time during the year. The $25,000 allowance begins to phase out as your modified adjusted gross income exceeds $100,000 ($50,000 if married filing separately) and is completely eliminated if your modified adjusted gross income is $150,000 or more ($75,000 if married filing separately). Modified adjusted gross income is your adjusted gross income without taking into account any allowable passive activity loss, rental real estate losses allowed for real estate professionals, taxable social security benefits and certain adjustments to income from page 1 of your Form 1040.

# Self Rentals and Passive Losses

You must be careful if you are involved in what is considered a self-rental situation. What is a self-rental? Here's what Treasury Regulation 1.469-2(f)(6) states:

Property rented to a non-passive activity. An amount of the taxpayer's gross rental activity income for the taxable year from an item of property equal to the net rental activity income for the year from that item of property is treated as not from a passive activity if the property—(i) Is rented for use in a trade or business activity (within the meaning of paragraph (e)(2) of this section) in which the taxpayer materially participates (within the meaning of § 1.469–5T) for the taxable year.

***Plain English Interpretation:*** If you have net rental income from property that you rented to a trade or business that you materially participated in, then the net rental income is considered non-passive and cannot be offset by passive losses. Let's look at an example of when this situation might occur. Let's say you have a limited partnership interest in a real estate venture that yields a net passive loss of $10,000 for the year. You also own a building that you operate your business from and your business pays rent. The net rental income from your building is $12,000. Generally you would be able to net the $10,000 passive loss against your $12,000 passive income and report net passive income on your tax return in the amount of $2,000. The self-rental rules however prevent you from characterizing your net rental income from your building rental as passive income because you rented it to your business. Therefore you cannot use the $10,000 in passive losses from your limited partnership interest. It's also worth noting that it is not necessary for you to own the business that is involved in the self-rental. The self-rental rules would apply if you materially participated in the business without any ownership.

# How To Audit-Proof Your Return

## Types of Audits

Even if you structure your business to lower your audit risk and even though audit rates are at historical lows, there is always a chance that your tax return will be selected for examination. Your best defense is to treat every tax return you file as if it were going to be audited.

Audits generally fall into two categories: correspondence audits and field audits. Correspondence audits are handled entirely by mail. This type of audit is common if a return was selected for examination because of a specific item and it can be resolved through telephone calls and submitting required documentation. Field audits are performed in person by revenue agents, tax compliance officers, tax examiners and revenue officers. These may be held at your home or place of business, your CPA's, enrolled agent's or attorney's office or even at a local IRS office. The IRS generally allows a taxpayer to be represented by a certified public accountant, an attorney or an enrolled agent. Regardless of the type of audit, your documentation requirements are the same.

## Documenting Your Tax Return

Documenting your tax return goes beyond having a receipt for an expense. Let's break it down into three areas.

**First you must be able to document your tax deductions.** Generally, the IRS does not require records in a specific format to substantiate general business expenses. You will have to be able to document what you paid and proof that you paid it. This can be accomplished with canceled checks, credit card receipts and even bank statements if they provide sufficient information. Here are some minimum requirements:

- Canceled checks must show the payee, amount, check number and date it cleared your account.
- Credit card receipts must show the payee, amount and date.

Business expenses for travel, entertainment and car expenses require more substantiation. Even if you have proof that you paid for an expense, you will have to establish what you paid if it is not clear from the receipt and what the business purpose was for the expenditure.

**Second, you may need to document what you did and in certain situations how many hours you spent doing it.** Passive activities and material participation have a 500 hour requirement. For real estate professional status there is a 750 hour requirement. In Chapter Ten: Beat Rising Medical Costs: Beyond Healthcare Savings Accounts, you learned you may establish a MERP for your non-business owner spouse that works for your business and establishing the work performed and the hours is key to upholding the bona fide business purpose of the MERP.

**Third, you should have an accounting system that pulls everything together;** your income, expenses and resultant profit or loss as well as the detailed transactions that back everything up.

Sound complicated? It doesn't have to be. When I first started my business, my only decision was whether to get a pocket size or full size desk planner along with an auto log for my glove compartment. Today the best thing you can do is to incorporate what ever technology you're currently using into your business lifestyle. Use what ever you're comfortable with, a computer or internet based calendar or a paper planner, and it doesn't take a huge investment. You can go to Google, Yahoo or a number of websites and sign up for free calendars and applications. Your calendar can serve to document the hours you spend on different activities and detailed notes will establish the underlying business purpose. You can include detailed notes about expenses incurred. At the last conference I attended, one person was taking a picture of a receipt with his cell phone and emailing it for later filing. You could use a scanner for archiving receipts and take advantage of "paperless statements" offered by most banks and credit card companies and download the statements without the need for scanning. A word of caution about "paperless statements"; most statements are available online for 18 to 36 months and this is usually not long enough for audit purposes so I always recommend you download PDF copies and store them on your computer or server.

As for an accounting system to pull it all together there are plenty of off the shelf and web-based, reasonably priced programs you could use. You should also consider outsourcing this function to a professional. I know there's a tendency to want to save money but as a business owner you're always better off doing what you do best and producing income rather than struggling with an administrative function you're probably not comfortable with. Outsourcing your accounting function will also ensure that your books are maintained on a routine basis and not just when you have time to take away from your business. It will serve to defend you from an audit and provide the ability to review your profit and loss statement on a periodic basis and make informed decisions about your business.

However you decide to document your write-offs, the best way to avoid being unprepared is to assume you *will* be audited. Behave as if every tax break you use will be examined under the scrutiny of the IRS. In the end, it's all about winning the game without breaking the rules!

# Ronald D'Arminio, CPA CTC

CEO & President
Ronald D'Arminio CPA P.C.
Randolph, New Jersey
www.NJCPA.pro

M r. D'Arminio is the President and founder of Ronald D'Arminio CPA P.C., a New Jersey based certified public accounting firm that specializes in helping business owners, real estate investors and individuals minimize their tax burden. Upon graduating college in 1984, he was employed by Ernst & Whinney, a National CPA firm. In 1988 Mr. D'Arminio became a small business owner himself. Since that time his practice has continually evolved to meet the needs of his clients. Mr. D'Arminio believes in building trust and relationships with his clients while delivering proactive tax planning services. For 27 years he has helped hundreds of business owners and individuals make more while keeping more of what they make.

Mr. D'Arminio received a Bachelor of Science in Business Administration from Montclair State College and a Master of Science in Taxation from Seton Hall University. In keeping with his commitment to his clients, Mr. D'Arminio was among the first CPAs in the State of New Jersey to attain the Certified Tax Coach designation. He is an active member of the American Institute of Certified Tax Coaches, an elite group of tax professionals that are committed to proactively plan and implement tax strategies for their clients. In 2011, Mr. D'Arminio was recognized as a 25 year member of the New Jersey Society of Certified Public Accountants and is also a member of the American Institute of Certified Public Accountants.

Mr. D'Arminio lives with his wife Erika and their sons Alex, Will and Eric in Roxbury Township, New Jersey where he is an active member of the community and has volunteered his time for several youth organizations including the Roxbury Football Fan Club Inc., Roxbury Recreation Field of Dreams Inc., Roxbury Little League and Roxbury Recreation Department.